MANHATTAN'S
TURTLE BAY

MANHATTAN'S TURTLE BAY

Story of a Midtown Neighborhood

Pamela Hanlon

ARCADIA
PUBLISHING

Published by Arcadia Publishing,
Charleston SC, Chicago IL, Portsmouth NH, San Francisco CA

Printed in the United States

Library of Congress control number: 2007937984

For all general information contact Arcadia Publishing at:
Telephone 843-853-2070
Fax 843-853-0044
E-Mail sales@arcadiapublishing.com
For customer service and orders:
Toll-Free 1-888-313-2665

Visit us on the Internet at www.arcadiapublishing.com

*Author's proceeds from the sale of this book are being donated to the Turtle Bay
Association.*

CONTENTS

ACKNOWLEDGMENTS

If a neighborhood can be judged by the kindness of its people, then surely Turtle Bay is the finest community around. Space doesn't permit mention of all those who played a role in gathering the story of Turtle Bay's past half-century. Some are included in the book itself, and others are noted in "Interviews and Conversations" in the Sources section on page 155.

Here, I would especially like to express my appreciation to John Detmold, whose mother, Mabel, and brother Peter were central to Turtle Bay's 20th-century history; Robert Moyer, whose remembrances of his days with James Amster in Amster Yard were invaluable in envisioning the neighborhood as it once was; Archibald and Marion King, who bought a Turtle Bay brownstone in the 1950s and whose memories of those early days were so enlightening; Jeannie Sakol, who first moved to Turtle Bay as a young writer in the 1950s and never left; and Bruce Silberblatt, whose knowledge of the community and whose advice and assistance throughout the project were much appreciated. And a special thanks to Bill Curtis, who has given a lifetime of service to the neighborhood as president of the Turtle Bay Association, and whose understanding of the area was invaluable in telling its story.

I also wish to thank others who provided valuable suggestions and help with the project—Olga Hoffmann, Millie Margiotta, Prue Bach Mortimer, Debra Pickrel, Buddy Radisch, and Erik Stapper. And much appreciation goes to Jim Kempert, editor at Arcadia Publishing, for his kind support and counsel.

Mostly, I wish to thank all the members of the Turtle Bay Association, the 50th anniversary of which was the inspiration for writing this story about Manhattan's East Midtown community since the mid-1950s.

PROLOGUE

"Do you live in New York?"

"Yes, ma'am."

"May I ask where?"

"In a house in Turtle Bay, ma'am, between the Waldorf
and the United Nations."

The Queen Mother was backstage at London's Haymarket Theatre to
receive the cast of *The Matchmaker* when she posed the question to the
show's star, American actress Ruth Gordon. Ms. Gordon's husband,
playwright Garson Kanin, who later wrote of his wife's reply, would
often say that they lived in "Turtle Bay, a small town in the great City
of New York."

It was the mid-1950s. And like so many theatrical, musical, and
literary figures, the couple had chosen the "small town" of Turtle
Bay as their home. They lived in a town house on East 49th Street,
next door to their good friend Katharine Hepburn, across the back
garden from essayist E. B. White, three blocks from Irving Berlin's big
house on the East River, and closer still to a promising young actress,
Joanne Woodward, who had recently moved into a brownstone on
East 51st Street.

In the more than half-century since then, the neighborhood has
continued to attract prominent and celebrated residents—actors,
musicians, and writers, as well as diplomats, professionals, and
wealthy entrepreneurs.

As Ms. Gordon's response to the Queen Mother so aptly portrayed, the neighborhood is nestled—some might say "squeezed"—between towering high-rise development that by the late 1950s was threatening to encroach still further. This is the story of the past 50 years of Turtle Bay, the people who have lived and worked there, and how they have strived to retain the community's "small town" character in the midst of the Manhattan metropolis.

MANHATTAN'S
TURTLE BAY

1. MID-CENTURY MAKEOVER: THE 1950S

I tell people that during my lifetime, I moved from the slums to the fashionable East Side without changing my address.
—Rita Carpanini, who was born in an apartment on East 49th Street in the 1930s and lived there until the 1970s.

THE EL COMES DOWN

Taverns up and down Manhattan's Third Avenue were packed on the afternoon of February 16, 1956, crowded with young people celebrating the end of an era.

Earlier in the day, a giant crane had yanked the last pillar of the Third Avenue El from its base, sending the rusty steel column crashing to the avenue at a spot just north of 42nd Street. Thousands of spectators were on hand to cheer. Scores of news photographers scrambled to get the best shot. City officials held yet another press briefing to tout their plans for the "new" Third Avenue. And the myriad saloons along the avenue opened their doors to reveling neighbors for what came to be known as "coming down" parties.

For the first time since August 1878, Third Avenue was out from under the dark, dirty shadow of the El, the last of a network of noisy elevated railroads that had once operated along four of Manhattan's avenues. Now, Third Avenue was about to be transformed. It was being widened, lighted, and landscaped. At 70 feet, it would be one of the city's broader avenues. New high-powered fluorescent lights would make it the brightest. And young London plane trees, to be planted every 40 feet along the whole stretch of the thoroughfare, would give it a fashionable flair.

While the entire seven-and-a-half-mile length of Third Avenue—from City Hall to 129th Street—was scheduled for a makeover, it was the Midtown blocks, between 42nd and 57th Streets, that were the center of attention. Indeed, city officials were calling the Midtown stretch of Third Avenue, long known for its saloons, pawn shops, and antique dealers, the future "gold coast" of Manhattan. Property values along the avenue were skyrocketing, and a frenzy of high-rise office construction already was under way.

Some wanted to rename the avenue to reflect its new status. Real estate developers and businessmen feared that unless Third Avenue was given a more distinctive name, it would forever reflect the image of its shabby past. "International Boulevard" and "The Bowerie," the name of Peter Stuyvesant's 1650s Manhattan farm, were early contenders. "Avenue of the Promenades" and "MacArthur Boulevard" were proposed later.

For months, both local and national media featured stories about the new avenue and its potential. "Will It Rank with Park?" a *New York Herald Tribune* headline asked, in one of a series of five articles on the new Third. Countless photo stories featured the modern glass office towers that soon would line the thoroughfare, along with profiles of the real estate developers building them. And almost daily, newspapers interviewed Third Avenue bar owners and small shopkeepers as they anxiously waited to learn if—more likely when—they would lose their leases, to be displaced by new development rising all around them.

For the neighborhood of Turtle Bay, bounded by Lexington Avenue and the East River from roughly 43rd Street to 53rd Street, the El's coming down was a pivotal event, representing one—but certainly not the only—monumental change taking place in the community in the mid-1950s.

Just east of Third Avenue, new high-rise apartment buildings were being planned. Sky-high real estate prices precluded all but commercial buildings directly on the avenue, but developers of residential buildings wanted to stay close to the Third Avenue action. And so old tenement buildings and brownstones on the crosstown streets and along Second Avenue were coming down, to be replaced with apartment buildings generally 15 to 20 stories tall.

At Turtle Bay's East River boundary, the United Nations headquarters was settling into its new 18-acre campus. Most of the buildings in the strikingly modern complex had been completed by 1952, but the library at the south end would not open until 1961. The United Nations Gardens had not yet been fully planted. Neighbors were still trying to adjust to the new name for the Midtown section of First Avenue, United Nations Plaza. And as the big world body became the city's number-one visitor attraction, crowds of tourists—and their buses—were a new feature in Turtle Bay.

The changing neighborhood now found itself at the center of the world's stage, in the midst of the city's biggest building boom and enjoying a thriving economy. Yet Turtle Bay was still a neighborhood of everyday concerns. And it would be another, less dramatic change—common to all of Manhattan and, indeed, the entire country—that would pose a unique challenge to Turtle Bay residents. A dilemma over increasing traffic and a threat to the neighborhood's tall shade trees would bring the people of Turtle Bay together in a way that would endure for decades to come.

In the 1950s, America's postwar love affair with the automobile was nowhere more visible than in Manhattan. By 1955, the number of cars entering and leaving Manhattan each workday had nearly doubled from the late 1940s, and streets were at times impassable. Amidst a long-running, though dying, debate over a proposed elevated crosstown expressway at 30th Street, the city introduced new tactics to deal with the traffic—from alternate-side-of-the-street parking to one-way traffic flows on more of the city's avenues.

But City Hall couldn't control the size of the new automobiles. Cars coming off Detroit's assembly lines in the mid-1950s were wider and longer each year. Midtown traffic tie-ups had become unbearable.

The Manhattan borough president's office came up with a plan. It wanted to widen six of Midtown's narrow crosstown streets to 36 feet, tearing up sidewalks and uprooting trees in the process. Widening the streets, it was argued, would provide enough room for two lanes of traffic, with parking at both curbs and comfortable leeway in between.

The streets slated for widening included two in Turtle Bay. East 49th Street and East 50th Street, both just over 30 feet wide, would lose sidewalk on each side, and their 40-foot honey locust and London plane trees would be destroyed. Four streets in the Murray Hill neighborhood were also on the schedule.

One of the residents on East 49th Street in the 1950s was a successful interior designer named James Amster. Amster had created a picturesque enclave of buildings around a courtyard and garden on the north side of the street between Second and Third Avenues. From a collection of 19th-century buildings that he bought in the 1940s, he had turned the complex into a home and office for himself, with another five apartments for such notable figures as decorator Billy Baldwin, sculptor Isamu Noguchi, and fashion designer Norman Norell.

He called it Amster Yard. One had only to peek into the courtyard, with its refined architectural detail and well-kept English garden, to know that the charismatic, spirited Amster was not going to remain silent while the city moved ahead with plans to tear up his tree-shaded block.

Amster was sure he could count on support from his neighbors to the south, residents of a group of European-inspired town houses on 48th and 49th Streets called Turtle Bay Gardens. Among those living in the Gardens at the time were some of Manhattan's most celebrated names—Katharine Hepburn, playwright Garson Kanin, his wife actress Ruth Gordon, and writer E. B. White.

In the fall of 1957, amid a flurry of news reports about the street widening, Amster and the longtime manager of the Gardens, Mabel Detmold, invited a small group of neighbors to Amster Yard to discuss how to thwart the city plan. Among them was Mabel Detmold's son Peter, whose real estate business specialized in the many mid-19th century brownstones lining Turtle Bay streets, and Marion King, who with her husband, Archibald, had recently purchased a brownstone down the street from Amster Yard. The Kings figured they would lose the front gate to their brownstone if the street was widened. "We were a determined group," Mrs. King recalls.

They all agreed that the "traffic tangle"—as Amster called it—had to be dealt with. But they were convinced the solution shouldn't require cutting up sidewalks and chopping down trees. "The key to solving the problem," Amster said, "is simply to enforce existing traffic regulations."

Over the coming months, Amster and his fellow 49th Street residents would find a most unlikely neighbor to help prove that he was right. The 17th Police Precinct had temporarily moved its station house into the elegant 1920s Efrem Zimbalist mansion just a few doors east of Amster Yard. The precinct's presence on the block would ultimately be the key to showing the city that there was indeed a less destructive way to solve the traffic problem than by bulldozer and steamroller.

This Place Called Turtle Bay: A Look Back

The Turtle Bay of the mid-1950s—with its new Third Avenue, stylish residential oases, and troubling "traffic tangle"—reflected a history of dramatic change dating back to colonial times. Then, rolling hills and quiet meadowland surrounded a crescent-shaped bay on the East River that ran from today's 45th Street to about 48th Street. By the early 1700s, the area was commonly referred to as Turtle Bay, although later opinions differed as to why. Some say the name came from the Dutch word *deutal*, to describe the bay's "curved blade" shape. Others say the name reflected a profusion of turtles found in the bay. A meandering stream—Turtle Creek to some, De Voor's Mill Stream to others—flowed southeasterly, emptying into the bay at the foot of what is now 47th Street.

Big farms and estates dotted the land. In the mid-1700s, Turtle Bay Farm was among the largest, bordered by Beekman Farm to the north, Kips Bay Farm to the south, and the old Eastern Post Road to the west. At about 50th Street and Second Avenue, a tiny span called the "Kissing Bridge" crossed over Turtle Creek.

In 1763, James Beekman of Beekman Farm built one of New York's most magnificent mansions on the high ground that is now the intersection of First Avenue and 51st Street. "Mount Pleasant," as he called it, gained notoriety during the Revolutionary War when Lord William Howe took it over as a command post for the British army. Nathan Hale, the patriot spy, was tried and sentenced to death in the greenhouse on the grounds.

By the early 1800s, the city limits were pushing northward from lower Manhattan, and the city laid out its straight-line street grid for the future. Gradually, new streets and avenues opened up, reaching north of 42nd Street by mid-century. The rolling farmland was broken up into building lots, and brownstone row houses—their big front stoops lined up side-by-side along the new streets—began to rise in the area.

Construction slowed during the Civil War, but resumed again in the late 1860s. By then, the street building in the area had caused the little Turtle Creek to back up, and the surrounding land became swampy, the water unhealthy. The bay was filled in and an underground drainage system was built, emptying into the East River at about 49th Street. Soon, the new landfill—now the grounds on which the United Nations stands—became an industrial site, taken over by stockyards, slaughterhouses, and breweries. A coal yard operated at the southern end of the Beekman property, a dumping ground ran from 46th to 47th Street along the riverbank, and shanties lined the hill to the south at what is now Tudor City. The area began a long period of decay.

Before long, Turtle Bay's brownstones were being converted into rooming houses for the growing number of immigrants working in the new industries on the landfill. The backyards of the tenements and brownstones, teeming with workers and their families, soon were filled with garbage cans and slop pails, and heavily laden clotheslines were strung from virtually every window.

When the elevated railroad began operating on Second and Third Avenues in the late 1800s, Turtle Bay's two important roadways turned noisy, dirty, and dark. This only added to the area's decline. For many years, Turtle Bay would be considered one of the least desirable sections of New York City.

It wasn't until 1919, when a wealthy New York socialite took a serious interest in New York's brownstones, that a "rebirth" of the area appeared possible. Charlotte Hunnewell Sorchan was a sophisticated, creative, and energetic woman in her late 40s who had traveled extensively in England, France, and Italy. She admired the Europeans' affinity for small squares of houses joined by a mutual garden. In New York, she'd observed, most brownstones had no room in front for a garden, and yet there was usually a small bit of land in the rear where, she said, "only dismal-looking linen might be seen flapping in the wind."

She began to imagine two rows of brownstones, back-to-back, joined by a lushly planted communal garden.

The idea had been suggested years earlier. In 1893, the *Real Estate Record and Guide* advocated for the creation of such gardens. But architects and builders of the time thought it impractical. Architect Charles Buek said it would be possible only if "some rich individual" would undertake it.

Almost 30 years later, Charlotte Sorchan would be that individual. She was indeed rich—she had inherited her wealth from her Bostonian parents who died when she was young—and she began a long search to find two uninterrupted rows of houses that could be redesigned with a central garden. She came upon 20 brownstones, but in an area that, according to her later writings, she considered "too far east." Still, she liked the houses—10 on 48th Street and 10 on 49th Street between Second and Third Avenues. Built in the early 1860s, their back lots even had a few old trees, including an especially large, graceful willow that she surmised was kept alive by waters from the Turtle Creek flowing underground.

"Naught venture, naught have," she said. And so she bought the brownstones and asked architects Edward C. Dean and William Bottomley, who later designed the exclusive River House on East

52nd Street, to alter them. No two were to be alike, except that all front stoops were removed, the kitchens were moved to the street side and the living spaces relocated to the back overlooking what would become a haven reminiscent of an Italian garden. The garden was formed by taking six feet of land from the rear of each lot to create a central garden path, leaving plenty of space for a private terrace directly in back of each house. A replica of the fountain that stands at the entrance to Rome's Villa Medici was placed in the center near the old willow tree, its rounded basin following the curvature of the tree's twisted trunk.

By the time the house renovations and garden were completed in 1921, Charlotte Sorchan had married a prominent New York surgeon, Dr. Walton Martin, and the newlyweds moved into the double-lot house at the western end of the 49th Street row, No. 228. They had a household staff of nine, and nine wood-burning fireplaces. Mrs. Martin then sold the other houses, at cost, through her new Turtle Bay Holding Company, and kept four houses to rent.

She called her creation Turtle Bay Gardens, and cast-iron turtles adorned many of its front gates. The Gardens quickly became a sensation and sparked a revitalization of the area. Soon, the real estate community was referring to the neighborhood that just years before had been considered "too far east" as the "*select* Turtle Bay Gardens district."

About the same time, much of East Midtown began to show signs of a renaissance. On Beekman Place at the river's edge, noted landscape architect Ellen Shipman started a trend with her conversion of an old brownstone, 19 Beekman Place, into an elegant Georgian-style home. In the newly named Sutton Place area, old houses were being bought and remodeled. And throughout the area, large new luxury apartment buildings were opening up in the late 1920s and 1930s. Soon, in 1942, the Second Avenue El came down; in 1947, the slaughterhouses and stockyards were cleared to make way for the United Nations; and finally, by 1956, the Third Avenue El was gone.

Turtle Bay was entering a new era.

THE WAY IT WAS IN THE 1950S

Jeannie Sakol was one of those who crowded into a tavern on the day in 1956 when the Third Avenue El came down. The young freelance writer joined friends at the corner of 44th Street and Third Avenue, at Costello's, run by brothers Tim and Joe and one of the most renowned of the avenue's many saloons. There, Sakol and her friends toasted Turtle Bay's future, rid of the El's shadows and noise. "It was a thrilling time to be in the neighborhood," says Sakol, who has lived in Turtle Bay for some 50 years. "I've had a life-long love affair with the area," she says.

But was Jeannie Sakol truly "thrilled" with the El's coming down? Like many others who had become accustomed to its shadows, Sakol admits to some nostalgia for the days of the elevated railroad. The avenue of "hock" shops, watering holes, and antique dealers under the rusty, rattling El had a certain appeal. "It was symbolic of old New York," she says. "I remember as a kid my father taking me on the Third Avenue El to go to Chinatown. You could practically reach out and touch the people in the old tenement buildings along the way."

Garson Kanin also hinted at mixed feelings about its demise. He once referred to the day "some wise guy made off with the Third Avenue El." An "irksome" change, he called it.

But Rita Carpanini didn't find it irksome. Born in the 1930s in a large tenement building, a "walk-up," on 49th Street east of Second Avenue, she and her friends avoided Third Avenue before the El came down. "It was too dark over there," she says of the shadowy street. She liked the way Turtle Bay was changing in the mid-1950s, and she stayed in the neighborhood—in the building where she was born—until 1971. "I tell people that during my lifetime, I moved from the slums to the fashionable East Side without changing my address," Carpanini says.

Peter Gabelli lived in the same walk-up. "It was a great block," says Gabelli, who stayed there for 65 years until he moved out in 2005. "So many kids on the street," he says of those baby-boom years in America. "I think we had 30 kids in our building alone."

In Turtle Bay in the 1950s, working class families rubbed shoulders with the rich and celebrated. Carpanini and Gabelli's tenement building stood less than a block from Katharine Hepburn's town house. The sidewalk in front of Hepburn's house had a nice incline, Carpanini recalls, "and when I was a little girl, my friends and I used to roller skate over there." She adds, "Sometimes we would peek in her windows to try to get a glimpse of her." (They did, once.) "When I grew up, and saw how politely she nodded when she passed neighbors on the street, I felt kind of badly about my childhood pranks," Carpanini says today.

Mrs. Peter's Sandwich Shoppe on Second Avenue between 49th and 50th Streets—where Mrs. Peter dished up spaghetti at her counter—was so popular with people in the neighborhood that some simply called it the "club." At Rocky Lee, another small Italian dining spot on Second Avenue, Gabelli—who worked as a building superintendent on Manhattan's West Side—remembers sitting next to actor Paul Newman and his new wife, actress Joanne Woodward. The couple lived in the East 50s. "We had a nice chat," Gabelli recalls, "and do you know, from that day forward whenever I saw Mr. Newman on the street, he would stop and talk with me. It was a real friendly neighborhood back then."

The area reflected a confident and optimistic New York City. The popular Mayor Robert Wagner was early in his first of three terms; Manhattanites were proud of their borough president, Hulan Jack, the highest-ranking black elected official in the country; and the city's economy was robust and growing. Nowhere was prosperity more evident than in Turtle Bay, with its El now down, new construction all around, and the United Nations drawing the neighborhood into the international spotlight.

Just a block from Mrs. Peter's homey eatery stood one of the top restaurants, and priciest, in all of Manhattan—Roger Chauveron's Chambord on Third Avenue between 49th and 50th Streets. Le Bistro, just up the avenue, joined a host of less expensive French eateries in the neighborhood, including Le Cave Henri IV on 52nd Street and Copain (later the location of a famous scene in the movie *The French Connection*) on First Avenue. Supper clubs were a trend in New York at the time, and two of Turtle Bay's finest were Gatsby's on First and The Living Room on Second.

Newsmen from the nearby *Daily News* and *Daily Mirror*, New York's popular tabloids, gathered at hangouts on 45th Street with names like Pen and Pencil, Press Box, and Scribes. Turtle Bay's "steak row" was famous: the Palm, Pietro's, Christ Cella, Manny Wolf's, and the biggest of them all, Danny's Hideaway on 45th Street, with its 11 dining rooms seating up to 300 people in three four-story buildings.

Neighbors shopped for their meat at Jack's on Second Avenue and for their fish at Tudor Fish Market on First. Do-it-yourselfers dropped by Richardson & Dutt's Lumber Yard or Jack and Walter Gasnick's Supply Company.

After school, kids took art and dance lessons at Grosvenor Neighborhood House, a settlement house on 49th Street between First and Second Avenues, or music classes at the long-established Turtle

Bay Music School. They met friends at Charlie Savio's soda fountain at the northwest corner of First Avenue and 49th Street, or—for the more daring among them—a special thrill was to sneak down to the basement of the old Emerald Café on Third Avenue at 48th Street to lift a manhole cover and drop a fishing line into the trickling branch of the Turtle Creek running below.

Living Among Stars

By the mid-20th century, the neighborhood had become well known as home to celebrities of stage and screen, and of the literary world as well. Maxwell Perkins, the legendary Scribner's editor, had been one of the first to move to Turtle Bay, living at 246 East 49th Street in Turtle Bay Gardens for many years. Across the garden, the influential journalist Dorothy Thompson made her home at 237 East 48th Street and the Botsford brothers—Stephen, president of the *New Yorker*, and Gardner, longtime *New Yorker* editor—both lived in Turtle Bay Gardens. William Jovanovich, president of Harcourt Brace & World, and the well-known literary agent Julian Bach Jr. called Turtle Bay home.

Perhaps best known among the neighborhood's bylines was that of essayist E. B. White. He and his wife Katharine lived at various times in Turtle Bay Gardens during the 1940s and 1950s, with their longest residency, 10 years, in a large two-story apartment they rented and remodeled at 229 East 48th Street. He often wrote of Turtle Bay in his *New Yorker* columns, and much of his correspondence, published in *Letters of E.B. White*, reflects his love of the Gardens and its greenery. In a springtime note to an aunt, he wrote: "Turtle Bay Garden is at its loveliest right now—full of tulips and blossoming shrubs, as well as a small but distinguished company of white-throated sparrows and hermit thrushes—transient visitors whose presence here seems miraculous."

From the rear windows of his duplex, White looked out over the decades-old willow tree, thriving with help from waters of the nearby Turtle Creek. It was the willow Charlotte Martin found there when she first bought the houses in 1919. And it was the tree that White would link with the city itself in his perceptive and now-famous essay *Here is New York*, first published in 1948. The Turtle Bay willow would take on renewed meaning for New Yorkers many years later—in 2001—when *Here is New York*, republished, provided some needed comfort to a city stunned and saddened by terrorist attacks.

Of the many musical luminaries in Turtle Bay in the 1950s, Irving Berlin was surely the most famous. He lived with his wife, Ellin, in an exquisite house at the southeast corner of Beekman Place and 50th Street. Considered one of the last significant private residences constructed in Manhattan, the house was built in the early 1930s for James V. Forrestal, investment banker and later secretary of defense. The Berlins had long admired the five-story house when, in 1946, the popular composer's huge Broadway success *Annie Get Your Gun* gave him the financial security to buy it.

Berlin moved in with three pianos: a Steinway upright for the paneled library on the ground level overlooking a terrace, a grand piano for the living room on the second floor, and a third piano for his top-floor workroom, where he also painted.

Neighbors saw little of the composer during the decade of the 1950s. Now in his 60s, Berlin had become semi-reclusive, and except for early morning or evening walks—when he believed he was less likely to be recognized—he was seldom spotted outside his house.

"Garbo sightings," on the other hand, were frequent. The film legend Greta Garbo lived on 52nd Street overlooking the East River. She strolled in the neighborhood almost daily, hidden behind the brim of her floppy hat and avoiding eye contact with anyone she passed. The

Third Avenue antique dealers all knew her well. At least twice a week, they said, she strolled down the avenue and into their shops under the El. When the El came down, she followed them to their new addresses nearby. "She didn't buy much," says Lewis Baer, who owns Newel Art Galleries and who as a young boy helped out in his grandfather's gallery on Second Avenue. "But she loved to look," he says, "and we loved to have her."

Through the years, the celebrity resident probably most beloved by her neighbors was actress Katharine Hepburn, not only because of her star status, but because she was such a lively, visible member of the community. She bicycled in the neighborhood, shopped in its small stores, shoveled snow from her front entrance, and carried firewood into her house in the winter and flowers and plants for her back garden in the summer.

Hepburn first rented her Turtle Bay Gardens town house, 244 East 49th Street, with her husband, Ludlow Ogden Smith, in 1932. In 1937, after she and "Luddy" had separated, she bought the four-story house, and still owned it at her death in 2003.

Hepburn spent much of her early career in Hollywood, but through the years the Turtle Bay house was the only residence she owned and the one where she felt most at home. "It's quiet and convenient and it's mine and I like it," Hepburn said in her 1991 autobiography, *Me.*

It was Katharine Hepburn who influenced friends Garson Kanin and Ruth Gordon to move to Turtle Bay.

Fresh from their Academy Award nomination for best screenplay for *Adam's Rib*, starring Hepburn and Spencer Tracy, Kanin and Gordon were feeling good about their careers in 1950 and had decided to buy a house. After a long search, they signed a contract on a place in

Greenwich Village. Shortly afterward, they had dinner with Hepburn, and told her of their plans.

"Nonsense," she said of the couple's decision. "You have to own something where the property values are sure to increase—like here—in Turtle Bay Gardens."

And so, Hepburn set out to find her friends a Turtle Bay town house.

She was friendly with her neighbors next door, at 242 East 49th Street. George Rublee and his wife had been original purchasers when the Gardens were first developed in the early 1920s. He had been an influential lawyer and foreign policy adviser to several presidents, from Woodrow Wilson to Franklin Roosevelt. Now elderly, the couple and Hepburn apparently came to agree that they should move to an apartment, easier for a couple their age. And Hepburn said she knew just the right buyers for their house.

Kanin later wrote that when he and his wife looked at the five-story Turtle Bay Gardens town house, they immediately fell in love with it and bought it—for exactly what Hepburn told them to offer—$58,000. The couple moved in on Christmas Eve 1951, and owned the house, next door to Hepburn, for some 40 years.

The Kanins hosted many small dinner parties, candlelit in their dining room overlooking the garden. "Celebrities were almost commonplace at the Gardens, by far the most numerous issued from the Kanins at 242," said writer Ned Calmer, who observed the action from his 49th Street apartment just west of the Gardens.

But of all their guests, Kanin liked to tell of Hepburn's "uninvited appearance."

It was in 1959, when the lyricists Betty Comden and Adolph Green were dining at 242. The conversation came around to Hepburn. "What kind of a neighbor is she, anyway?" Comden asked. "Does she come in and borrow a cup of sugar once in a while?"

Suddenly, the kitchen door opened, and Hepburn was standing in front of them wearing a big wig and carrying two others. "What do you think of this?" she said, modeling one of the wigs for an upcoming play. "Oh hell, you can't see in this silly candlelight. Put some lights on," she said, and then turned up the lights herself.

Finally noticing other people in the room, Hepburn smiled. "Nice to have met you," she said, and exited quickly to her house next door.

Ruth Gordon turned to Betty Comden: "Does that answer your question?"

The Wrong Side

"It was on the wrong side of the tracks," Melvyn Kaufman says of a big parcel of land on Third Avenue that his family's development firm acquired in 1952. Indeed, when the Kaufman Organization, then headed by Melvyn's father William, first looked at the full blockfront between 44th and 45th Streets on the avenue's *east* side, the El was still thundering overhead, with no date set for demolition. The avenue of dark taverns and dingy tenements didn't look promising to most. But the Kaufmans took a chance on the avenue's potential and built what would be their first high-rise office building in Midtown.

Melvyn Kaufman and his brother Robert were just getting started in their father's business in the early 1950s. "You know, Pop, this isn't going to fly unless we do something to catch people's attention," Melvyn told his father. "We need a great architect."

The great architect turned out to be the modernist—and Turtle Bay resident—William Lescaze. The Swiss-born Lescaze lived at 211 East 48th Street, in an 1850s brownstone that he had converted into a modern, International-style home and office in the 1930s. (Today, the house—a New York City landmark and listed on the National Register of Historic Places—is owned by Melvyn and Robert Kaufman.)

Lescaze designed a 19-story, 500,000-square-foot office building for the Kaufmans' site, to be known by its address, 711 Third Avenue. Construction began well before the El came down.

"Lescaze told me, 'You can't just let it go up. You need to give it some color . . . some life,' " Melvyn Kaufman recalls.

Lescaze provided the color: The building's 11-story brick tower atop its white base is blue. As for the "life," the Kaufmans commissioned the abstract painter Hans Hofmann to design a gigantic Venetian mosaic wrapping the lobby's elevator core. And sculptor Jose de Rivera created a striking stainless steel sculpture, "Continuum," that hangs at the building's entrance.

The concepts were revolutionary at the time. "Nobody was putting up a blue building, nobody was putting art in their buildings," says Melvyn Kaufman.

Almost immediately, 711 Third Avenue was a success. It was fully rented by the time it was completed in 1956, and architectural critics liked it.

Today, the Kaufmans are credited with pioneering the development of Third Avenue by being the first to cross over to the "wrong" side of the street even before the El came down. And the building's innovative and artful touches became a hallmark of Melvyn Kaufman's later buildings that featured outdoor plazas and whimsical art, much of it along Turtle Bay's stretch of Third Avenue.

GIRL SCOUTS ARRIVE

Other commercial developers soon followed the Kaufmans to Third. The avenue that was once said to have "more Irish bars than all of Dublin" was rapidly losing its convivial saloons to executive offices for banks, publishers, and advertising agencies. By 1959, according to one estimate, more than a quarter of the avenue's bars had been displaced. One disgruntled bartender is said to have told a reporter, "First thing you know, the Girl Scouts will be moving in."

They did. In fact, the Girl Scouts Building, the Scouts' headquarters at 830 Third Avenue until 1992, was the next to go up after the Kaufman's 711. Completed in 1957, the Skidmore, Owings & Merrill building was only 13 stories high, but the structure of glass curtain walls was highly regarded by the architectural community.

Only three more office buildings—630, 750, and 730—were completed on Third Avenue above 42nd Street during the 1950s. But by the early 1960s, office construction was booming.

Interest in residential development in Turtle Bay lagged behind commercial building. But late in the decade, new apartment buildings started rising, joining the area's older residential buildings that had gone up in the late 1920s and 1930s. The new apartments were typically of white or yellow brick construction. One, the 21-story Turtle Bay House, rose at the northwest corner of Second Avenue and 48th Street. Its marketing campaign boasted that its west-facing windows would overlook the lovely Turtle Bay Gardens.

The potential for "prying eyes" from apartments high above was not greeted warmly by Gardens residents. Katharine Hepburn, for one, was said to have considered moving.

She stayed, of course. And when the new corner apartment building opened in 1958, residents of the Gardens began to realize it would prove to be a "good neighbor." It actually improved the Gardens' security by serving as a barrier to intruders. And as for curious eyes, the Gardens' thick canopy of foliage blocked all but the most persistent among them.

As neighbors learned to live with construction cranes and new high-rise buildings, they turned their attention back to the threat of street-widening on East 49th and 50th Streets.

TACKLING THE TRAFFIC TANGLE

In the spring of 1958, Manhattan Borough President Hulan Jack's plan to ease traffic congestion by widening two Turtle Bay streets and four in Murray Hill awaited a final decision by the city's Board of Estimate, responsible for land use matters at the time.

The small group of neighbors who first met in Amster Yard in late 1957 continued to strategize on how to save their tree-lined blocks. To give their cause a higher profile, they had formed an organization, the East 49th Street Association, and asked James Amster—"Jimmy" to his neighbors and friends—to serve as chairman.

Amster continued to believe the traffic tangle could be alleviated if parking regulations were properly enforced. But now he was going to have to prove it, and soon, lest the board move ahead to cut up sidewalks and uproot trees.

Down the block from Amster Yard stood a lovely Tudor-style mansion at 225–227 East 49th Street. Designed by Grosvenor Atterbury in 1926 for the Russian émigré violinist Efrem Zimbalist and his wife, opera singer Alma Gluck, the 20-room house with its distinctive casement windows had fireplaces in almost every room, 11 bathrooms, stained-glass door panels, and an Italian garden out back. On the second floor a large music room featured dark wood floor-to-ceiling paneling, an ornately carved fireplace, and parquet floors.

Now, the house vacant, the 200 police officers of the 17th Precinct had come to stay for three years, until their new station house being built on East 51st Street was ready for occupancy.

They moved into the Efrem Zimbalist House in December 1957. The music room served as the officers' locker room. The large dining room that opened out onto the garden housed the precinct's front desk. The elaborate wallpaper got a coat of "municipal green" paint. And a temporary "17th Precinct" sign now shared space with a delicate violin coat of arms that Zimbalist had designed for the front entrance.

That spring, with traffic on his street seemingly worse each day, Amster asked Peter Detmold, the young realtor, to look into the problem. Along with Marion King, Detmold formed a committee to keep track of illegally parked cars on 49th Street between Second and Third Avenues. Strict enforcement of parking regulations at the time prohibited all daytime parking on the street on weekdays.

The committee members were precise and persistent. From May 15 to June 13, they counted 922 illegally parked cars. Many, they discovered, were owned by police officers who, like many workers in the area, drove to work and parked on the street near their temporary station house. That explained why the street's traffic congestion had recently worsened, and it would help Amster prove his point: Illegal parking was behind the traffic tie-ups.

Detmold and his neighbors enlisted the help of the police in clearing the streets, calling the Efrem Zimbalist House whenever they spotted an illegally parked car, and persisting until it was ticketed or moved. Then they called the Highway Department to send someone to observe the improved traffic flow once parking regulations were being enforced.

The illegal parking controversy became a major issue throughout Midtown, and in November 1958, a *New York Times* editorial called the situation a "disgrace" and asked, "Where are the police? Where is the Mayor?"

Detmold responded with a letter to the *Times*, applauding the editorial and detailing his committee's work on 49th Street. "While we have hardly won our battle . . . since our campaign began, there have been times when the street has been bare," he wrote.

Detmold's mother, Mabel, manager of Turtle Bay Gardens, told the parking story in a more personal way. Writing a few years later, she recounted how Charlotte Hunnewell Martin, the wealthy doctor's wife who had created Turtle Bay Gardens in 1920 and lived there ever since, coped in the late 1950s:

> When they [Dr. and Mrs. Martin] came to the Gardens to live, the city enjoyed a more relaxed way of life than it does today. Forty-ninth Street then was a far cry from today's crowded expressway. The Martins' distinguished old Lincoln would stop before the door of their house; the chauffeur would ring the door bell to alert the servants and return to the car to help his passengers alight. At this same curbstone in the twenties, cars often stood—although rarely unattended—while their owners were enjoying a musicale in the beautiful home of Efrem Zimbalist and Alma Gluck, across the street. By [the late 1950s], this had become the temporary headquarters of the Precinct 17 of the city's finest. . . . so many parked cars lined the street that it was sometimes necessary to stop in front of the police station, where there was always curb space available. Thus it was not unusual for Mrs. Martin to have a uniformed escort accompany her to her door, for a lady in her late eighties found the crossing very hazardous.[1]

Just days after the *Times* editorial and Detmold's letter, Police Commissioner Stephen Kennedy ordered that the "unwholesome parking abuses" in Midtown be cleaned up before the year-end holiday season. Throughout the city, the situation began to improve. Along 49th Street, empty curb lanes soon became the norm.

Soon, the Board of Estimate decided to start the street-widening project with just two streets, Murray Hill's 36th and 37th Streets, considered priorities because they carried the heaviest traffic flows between the Lincoln and Queens-Midtown tunnels. That Turtle Bay blocks were spared in the first phase was of no comfort to its residents, who knew their streets could be next. So the East 49th Street Association went to work to help Murray Hill in its fight.

The high-profile battle with the city continued into the summer of 1959. Members of the association repeatedly appeared before the board and at community meetings to support Murray Hill. "Using the 49th Street block between Second and Third Avenues as a test area, we have demonstrated that our streets can handle all the traffic required," Amster said. "Thus at what cost to city and resident alike do we contemplate turning our streets into glorified parking lots and truck causeways?"

At meeting after meeting, the Board of Estimate delayed action. Not until January 1961 did residents finally win their struggle when, by a unanimous vote, the board rejected the plan. The "old demon street-widening," as Amster called it, would surface from time to time in other parts of the city, but none of the Murray Hill or Turtle Bay crosstown streets was ever seriously threatened again.

Two years later, the *New York Times* wrote about the East 49th Street Association's campaign to stop illegal parking, in a story headlined "Parking Tickets Preserve Trees." It said the Turtle Bay neighbors' campaign to preserve their sidewalks and trees was so effective that "it caused officials of the Traffic, Police and Highway Departments to marvel at community determination and to wish at times for a little complacency."

Over the years, Turtle Bay residents would be anything but complacent. With Peter Detmold's diligence and Jimmy Amster's persuasiveness, the neighborhood would continue to work to maintain its small-town feel amidst the rising towers looming all around.

2. Recognizing Change: The 1960s

It's got personality, and people who really care about it.
—Composer Stephen Sondheim speaking about Turtle Bay, his home since 1960.

Towers Rise

The Turtle Bay neighborhood had its own movie theater in 1960—a grand house with 2,500 seats, a Beaux-Arts interior, an elegant staircase leading to three balconies, and four tiers of boxes overlooking an enormous stage. Located at the southeast corner of 51st Street and Lexington Avenue, the theater was built by Oscar Hammerstein in 1914 as an opera house. But when it opened, it almost immediately began offering vaudeville and films because a dispute with the Metropolitan Opera Company kept Hammerstein (grandfather of lyricist Oscar Hammerstein II) from staging opera there. He soon sold the theater to Marcus Loew, and it became known as Loew's Lexington Theatre.

Loew's Lexington was the site of many star-studded screenings over the years. Some neighbors remember that Marilyn Monroe and Arthur Miller, who lived on nearby Sutton Place, created such a stir when they arrived for a showing of *Some Like it Hot* that police had to be called in.

On Sunday, April 3, 1960, Loew's Lexington showed its last movie. The next day, demolition crews were on the site and ground soon was broken for a new building.

Unlike construction on Third Avenue, this would *not* be an office tower. Laurence and Preston Robert Tisch, whose lodging company had invested in the Loews Theatre chain, hired architect Morris Lapidus to design a hotel, the Summit. Lapidus was best known for his two elaborate hotels in Miami Beach, the Fontainebleau and the Eden Roc. Now, he created a 21-story hotel of pale turquoise glazed brick in the form of an "S"—a squiggle, he called it. It was almost universally disliked by architecture critics and neighbors alike. "It would look better closer to the beach," was a common joke around Turtle Bay. Its tall vertical sign was said to be more appropriate to a suburban motel than a Turtle Bay hotel, and its multi-colored lobby design was referred to as "tongue-in-cheek Aztec." Indeed, within three months of its opening in 1961, Lapidus was asked to re-design the lobby, which he promptly did, in tones of brown and tan. "Color was just too much for New Yorkers accustomed to the dirty, grimy grays," he quipped.

Over on Third Avenue, the office building frenzy was in high gear. All told, nine high-rise office towers opened on the Turtle Bay stretch of the avenue in the 1960s. Among them was a second Third Avenue building by the Kaufman group, 777, completed in 1963 on the east blockfront between 48th and 49th Streets. It had been the site of several old tenement buildings, including one housing the neighborhood's popular Richardson & Dutt's Lumber Yard. When the 38-story 777 building was officially named the Plywood Building—for its primary tenant, the U.S. Plywood Corporation—most neighbors assumed it was a nod to their favorite old lumber store.

The Plywood Building proved a handsome addition to the avenue. Like the Kaufmans' first building on Third, 711, this too was designed by William Lescaze and was the first building constructed under the city's 1961 Zoning Resolution, which gave developers floor-area "bonuses" in return for public outdoor plazas. The 777 building had

16-foot setbacks on all street sides, outdoor public seating, a Beverly Pepper sculpture at its entrance, and Theodore Ceraldi's "Big Red Swing"—in the shape of a grand piano lid—at the 49th Street corner. A nearby grove of trees was planted in a bed shaped as a mirror image of the swing.

Two other Kaufman towers were built on Third Avenue in later years, the 39-story 767, a curved tower of brick and glass, and the 37-story 747. In putting up 747 in 1972, on the east blockfront between 46th and 47th Streets, the Kaufmans were forced to build around a venerable old restaurant, one of the last holdouts among the many establishments that had operated under the clattering El. First opened in 1915, Joe and Rose Restaurant had served as a speakeasy during Prohibition. Now, owner Rose Resteghini refused to sell the five-story building unless her ground-floor restaurant remained undisturbed. So the Kaufmans took down the top four floors of the tenement and left the Italian steakhouse in its original condition. For more than 15 years, until it closed in the late 1980s, Joe and Rose continued to serve patrons within the walls of the new office tower surrounding it.

The Durst Organization rivaled the Kaufmans in the early development of Third Avenue. The group built four office towers along the avenue in the 1960s—733, 675, 825, and 757—along with 655 Third Avenue, at 42nd Street, in 1957. Seymour Durst, the firm's founder, lived in Turtle Bay in a brownstone on East 48th Street. In later decades, in the 1970s and 1980s, he would become a strong neighborhood supporter and active in community affairs.

Durst, who died in 1995, was well known for his impressive collection of old New York photos and historical material. So extensive was his collection—it eventually included 9,000 book titles, 3,000 glossy photos, and 20,000 postcards—that he said the only reason he eventually moved from Turtle Bay was because his collection simply "outgrew" his brownstone. Indeed, neighbors recall seeing his photos stored in a bathtub and in his refrigerator. Durst would explain that he didn't need the refrigerator. "I dine out," he would say.*

Meanwhile, the makeover continued on First Avenue, where probably the area's greatest transformation had taken place when industrial blight was razed to make way for the United Nations. Much of the Midtown stretch of the avenue was now officially known as United Nations Plaza, although most neighbors continued to call it by its numerical name.

On the east side of First Avenue, the low, swoop-roofed Dag Hammarskjold Library at the corner of 42nd Street—the last of the buildings on the U.N. campus—was completed in the fall of 1961. On the avenue's west side, new construction was in its early stages. Old tenements and warehouses were coming down to make way for office buildings, generally between 12 and 20 floors. Lescaze designed the Church Peace Center at the southwest corner of 44th Street, a work highly regarded for its compatibility with the United Nations. And farther north along the west side of the avenue were the U.S. Mission to the United Nations, the Institute of International Education, the Carnegie Endowment for International Peace (later headquarters of the Anti-Defamation League), and the Engineering Societies Center.

The Dollhouse

In 1960, Mabel Detmold marked her 25th year managing the town houses of Turtle Bay Gardens. Before she'd taken the Gardens job, she'd been a nurse and worked in the office of Dr. Walton Martin,

---

* Today, much of Durst's collection is available to the public at the Seymour B. Durst Old York Library and Reading Room at the Graduate Center of the City University of New York.

a physician who practiced in the Turtle Bay Gardens home where he lived with his wife Charlotte. Over the years, Mrs. Detmold came to enjoy the Gardens' ambience, affluence, and celebrity. And so, when Dr. Martin retired from his practice in 1935, she happily agreed to take over management of the Gardens. She converted his doctor's quarters into a full-time real estate office and became the "guardian" of the 20 elegant houses and their communal backyard.

After Dr. Martin died in 1949, followed by his widow Charlotte in 1961, Mrs. Detmold retired. Now in her 70s, she turned over her Gardens duties to her son Peter. For once, after a busy life as mother, nurse, and real estate manager, she had some free time. Her son John wanted her to write a book.

"I wish you'd start to put down on paper . . . some of the Turtle Bay story," John said in a letter from his home in California. "No one could tell this story except you." And so Mrs. Detmold started to write. She wrote about Charlotte Martin's search for the houses in 1919 and their alterations. But mostly, she wrote the story of the people who had lived in the houses—house biographies, she called them. She told of Broadway star Mary Martin, her husband Richard Halliday, and mother-in-law living at No. 233; Harry Belafonte rehearsing at his agent's apartment in the same house; June Havoc's blossoming acting career while she lived at No. 229; Tallulah Bankhead and her cheetah house-hunting at No. 241; and editor Maxwell Perkins meeting in his study at No. 246, in what were known to be rowdy quarrels, with the young writer Thomas Wolfe, who lived nearby at the Eastbourne (now 865 United Nations Plaza). They were straightforward accounts. But clearly, she kept some stories to herself. "It would have been fun to have told the truth about some of these people," she once wrote to John.

Mrs. Detmold died in 1964, only a few weeks after completing her manuscript. John Detmold arranged to have *The Brownstones of Turtle Bay Gardens* printed, and it was sold to raise funds for the East 49th Street Association. The frontispiece of the little book is Mrs. Detmold's own pen-and-ink drawing of the Gardens' old willow tree.

When the novelist Kurt Vonnegut moved to the neighborhood years later, in 1973, his brownstone faced the 48th Street side of the Gardens. On reading Mrs. Detmold's book, he wrote to John, an old college friend, that the book was like "an exquisite dollhouse. I get to peek through window after window, and there is always something cozy going on in there."

Celebrating Early Landmarks

As Mabel Detmold was writing of her "dollhouse" in the early 1960s, the monumental Pennsylvania Station on Manhattan's West Side was coming under the wrecker's ball. The controversial demolition started on October 28, 1963, and by the time it ended in 1966, the public outcry had led to passage of the city's first Landmarks Preservation Commission Law. In the future, city buildings and districts with "architectural, cultural, or historic" significance could be protected from being torn down or altered. Under the new law, once a property or district was named a landmark, it could not be significantly altered without city approval. Mayor Robert Wagner appointed an 11-member commission to consider proposed sites for "New York City Historic Landmark" status.

With new construction all around, Turtle Bay's appreciation for its historic buildings was growing. So when Turtle Bay Gardens' residents joined together to suggest their 20 houses be given landmark status as a historic district, the whole neighborhood applauded. And when

Philip Johnson, the eminent architect and friend of Jimmy Amster, urged Amster to propose Amster Yard as a landmark, the interior designer readily agreed.

The two Turtle Bay sites were among the first to be considered under the new law and on August 16, 1966, the commission announced that landmark status had been granted to both.* In selecting Turtle Bay Gardens, the commission said the houses with a central garden shared by the residents was "a fine example of cooperation and understanding among neighbors . . . a planning ideal which sets an example for the rest of the city." Amster Yard, the commission noted, "contains one of New York's most beautiful inner courtyards" and its remodeled old buildings combine to create "a harmonious and attractive group, of which the city may be proud."

Amster was elated with the landmark status. And he celebrated just as he had 20 years earlier when he first introduced Amster Yard to New York society: He gave a party. It was a gala affair for hundreds of friends, neighbors, and clients. His 1946 guest list had been illustrious, but this time around it was truly dazzling. In the intervening years, Amster had become a highly successful decorator and was well known in the city's social circles. His clients included both halves of Broadway's brilliant musical team Oscar and Dorothy Hammerstein and Richard and Dorothy Rodgers; as well as Vladimir Horowitz, Alan Jay Lerner, and Jessica Tandy and Hume Cronyn. And he had designed Peacock Alley, the lobby restaurant at the Waldorf-Astoria Hotel; redone the interiors for two ocean liners of Swedish

---

* In 1983, Turtle Bay Gardens Historic District was also added to the National Register of Historic Places.

American Lines; and been a featured designer in *House & Garden*, *House Beautiful*, and *Architectural Digest*.

Now he was celebrating his own home. Amster had first set eyes on what would become Amster Yard back in 1944 when, after a dinner party, two other guests who were in the real estate business took him to see some "down-in-the-heels properties," as he called them. An old tenement, boarding house, and a carpenter's workshop ringed a debris-filled yard. But the creative Amster immediately saw potential in the site. Adding to its allure was the fact that the location had once served as a stagecoach stop on the old Eastern Post Road, the Manhattan stretch of the Boston Post Road. Amster bought the dilapidated structures. He asked two friends, architect and painter Harold Sterner and art director Ted Sandler, to create a garden complex surrounded by offices and apartments renovated from the shells of the original buildings.

Within two years, on a May evening in 1946, Amster was ready to unveil his charming Amster Yard with a grand party attended by some 700 clients, friends, and the press. Eugenia Sheppard, writing for the *New York Herald Tribune*, described her gracious and handsome host as "a man with great romantic flair" and Amster Yard as "pretty and perfect . . . inside and out."

Guests entered through an archway leading from a street-side façade done in Federal eclectic style to a courtyard surrounded by painted brick walls, iron grillwork, hanging lamps, slate walkways, and lush landscaping. The longest space in the L-shaped courtyard was extended still further with a "visual trick," an eight- by five-foot framed mirror, a fascinating element suggested to Amster by his friend, the pioneering interior decorator Elsie de Wolfe. (Ms. de Wolfe, then 80 years old, was a guest at the party.)

It was Amster's dream to make Amster Yard a center of the design profession, and the earliest residents of its six apartments included the Yard's architect, Sterner, and his wife, Paula; art patron Leonard

Hanna; Billy Baldwin; Isamu Noguchi; Norman Norell; as well as Amster, of course. Amster, Sterner, and Baldwin also had business offices in the complex.

Quiet by day, Amster Yard came to life in the evenings with countless memorable parties. Amster liked festive, formal affairs, with cocktails in the courtyard and sit-down dinners in his drawing room. Some parties were themed—waiters dressed as French sailors for Bastille Day or guests in costume for an Arabian Nights gala ball. But it was not only large gatherings that Amster enjoyed. It was his custom to reserve at least one night a week for small sit-down dinners for six or eight friends and neighbors.

Always, he encouraged neighborhood get-togethers. "We need to bring a little community spirit to this part of Manhattan," he would say. In the 1960s, it became a popular Christmas tradition to gather for caroling in the Yard, followed by singing along Midtown streets and hot wassail in the Turtle Bay Gardens. (When the event attracted more than 400 carolers one year, Gardens residents complained and the tradition came to a quiet end.)

Serious issues were taken up at meetings in the Yard. As chairman of the Prescott Neighborhood House and its day care center, Amster hosted many of the organization's board meetings in the Yard. And as founder of the East 49th Street Association, he often held the association's business sessions there.

Among visitors to the Yard in those years was a young composer and lyricist, Stephen Sondheim, who had just bought his first home, a town house in Turtle Bay Gardens.

SIDE-BY-SIDE

In 1960, with his neighbors complaining of loud piano music from his rental apartment on East 80th Street, 30-year-old Stephen Sondheim

45

decided it was time to look for a new place. After a friend gave him what he calls an "economics" lesson in real estate—and realizing that the royalties from the recent success of *Gypsy*, his second Broadway hit, could help him afford a down payment—he started to think about buying.

It was a chance meeting with Anita Ellis, a well-known singer at the time and sister of Larry Kert, who played the lead role of Tony in Sondheim's first Broadway success, *West Side Story*, that led him to Turtle Bay Gardens. "Anita told me she and her husband were about to rent a triplex in a house at 246 East 49th Street, but she'd just found out the deal might fall through because the owners were thinking of selling the house instead," Sondheim remembers.

"So I called Peter Detmold of Detmold Realty," he says, "And Peter told me, 'That house isn't even on the market.' " Still, Detmold promised to let Sondheim know if it were put up for sale.

It wasn't long before Sondheim had signed a contract to buy the five-story house. He lived on the first two floors, and Anita Ellis and her husband rented the top three. "That helped me pay the mortgage," Sondheim recalls. In 1973, Sondheim stopped being a landlord and took over the entire house as his own. By that time, he had written music and lyrics for four Broadway hits—*A Funny Thing Happened on the Way to the Forum, Anyone Can Whistle, Company*, and *Follies*—and had picked up the first two of his seven Tony awards.

Sondheim's new house was directly to the east of Katharine Hepburn's longtime home. Did he know he was buying next door to Hepburn? Well, if he didn't, he soon found out. "One night before the sale closed, I took some friends over to look at the house," says Sondheim. "We walked out into the central garden, turned around and looked up, and there facing us through the window was Katharine Hepburn . . . and at that moment a pair of big broad arms reached around to embrace her. . . . Unmistakably, Spencer Tracy," he recalls.

Thus began many years of living "side-by-side" with Hepburn. Like his neighbor, Sondheim enjoyed bicycling. "It's half window-shopping, half riding in a car," he says. His friend Anthony Perkins got him into biking when, just a few years after Sondheim moved to 49th Street, Perkins gave him a bike for Christmas. "I came home one Christmas Eve to find a bike outside the house here on 49th Street, all wrapped up with a big ribbon."

Neighbors remember Sondheim on his bike, shopping in Turtle Bay, commuting to the theater district, and even continuing to ride after a bike accident left him with two broken ribs. Finally, in the mid-1970s, he put away his city bike when friends convinced him that worsening Midtown traffic posed too great a risk.

From the start, Sondheim was a supportive neighbor, joining the East 49th Street Association and offering his help whenever needed. "I've always loved our neighborhood," he says, "It's got personality, and people who really care about it."

Indeed, the area's "personality" was blossoming in the 1960s, attracting attention throughout the city with new restaurants, shops, and even a "factory." In 1963, Andy Warhol opened The Factory, his first studio, in what was then a loft building at 231 East 47th Street. For years, the lavish place—used by the artist to produce silk screens by day and for notorious superstar parties at night—was the most exciting place to be, and be seen, in all of New York.

Upscale shops were finding their way to Turtle Bay in the early 1960s. George and Effie Sotor opened Greek Island Limited, selling hand-made Greek accessories, in Amster Yard. "Chic Greek," Jimmy Amster called it. Greek Island quickly became a favorite with celebrity shoppers, including Jacqueline Kennedy, who stopped by when she was First Lady, and who later—after she married Greek shipping magnate Aristotle Onassis—was said to be a regular.

In 1961, Sidney and Phyllis Lucas moved their antiquarian print gallery, one of the city's oldest, to a new Turtle Bay location, at Second Avenue and 52nd Street. Lucas Gallery was the first North American publisher of Salvador Dali images, and the Spanish surrealist painter often visited the shop.

The same year, Chef Andre Soltner came from Paris to open his soon-to-be legendary Lutece in a brownstone on East 50th Street. For decades, many would consider Lutece the finest French restaurant not only in New York, but throughout the country. In 1966, the 90-year-old Billy's Restaurant, complete with its signature mahogany bar, moved to First Avenue near 52nd Street, its clientele a virtual "Who's Who" of New York. On East 49th Street, the Italian restaurant Antolotti's became a favorite. Novelist Truman Capote, who lived a block away on First Avenue, often was seen there, always at his preferred banquette along Antolotti's east wall. Soon, Paul Paolini—who bought the Efrem Zimbalist House once used as the 17th Precinct's temporary station house—took over Louise Jr. on 53rd Street, turning it into a comfortable Italian restaurant, one of the area's most popular.

All over Turtle Bay, residents' pride in the neighborhood was growing, and with it a desire to become involved. By 1965, the East 49th Street Association membership had grown from a handful of neighbors to more than 500, from streets far beyond 49th. And so in early 1965 the members adopted a new name. The Turtle Bay Association, the TBA, was formally introduced.

CHALLENGES AHEAD

The newly-named association had barely enough time to redesign its letterhead when it was confronted with its next big challenge. On July

19, 1965, a front-page headline in the *New York Times* announced: "Seven Garages Planned by City in Midtown." Accompanying the story was a Midtown map that shocked Turtle Bay neighbors. One of the sites planned for a municipal short-term parking garage was the full blockfront between 47th and 48th Streets on the west side of Second Avenue. A collection of old buildings housing shops and galleries was to be razed to make way for a multi-level 500-car garage.

Turtle Bay residents went into action. "In a neighborhood where there is heavy foot traffic along the sidewalks . . . the pedestrian is not merely ignored by this type of so-called planning; he is nearly trampled under foot," Peter Detmold wrote, as part of a resolution passed by the Turtle Bay Association.

Within a few months, the Site Selection Board of the City Planning Commission had received some 600 letters protesting the Turtle Bay garage and the traffic congestion it would cause. Turtle Bay was joined by protests against the garages throughout the city, and, with a change in mayoral administrations in January 1966—from Robert Wagner, who favored the garage plan, to John Lindsay, who campaigned against it—no garage was ever built on the site.

Detmold was fast becoming a leading voice in community affairs. Not only was he standing up for his own neighborhood's interests, but he was a staunch supporter of tenants' rights citywide. A persuasive debater, he frequently spoke out publicly on behalf of renters in their battles with landlords and commercial interests. And he was ever-protective of Manhattan's historic buildings, particularly in Turtle Bay, where he vigorously fought pressure from real estate developers who coveted the convenient Midtown address. In 1969, he told the *New York Times*, "Why, I've had serious city planning people tell me that it's obscene to keep a brownstone on land as valuable as the lots in Turtle Bay. Obscene, that's the word they use."

Detmold had moved to Turtle Bay in 1952, a Cornell University Phi Beta Kappa with undergraduate and graduate degrees in medieval history, with a minor in music. In 1943, in his sophomore year, he interrupted his studies to join the Army. He served as a sergeant in the 87th Infantry Division, fighting with a mortar section in the Battle of the Bulge and earning a Bronze Star before returning to Cornell to resume his studies in 1945.

Detmold's love of classical music had brought him to New York in search of a career in the music industry. But when he first arrived, he started working in his mother Mabel's real estate office at Turtle Bay Gardens. He liked the work and soon took over the business, specializing in the sale and rehabilitation of old brownstone row houses.

In 1963, a young graphic artist walked into the Detmold Realty office looking for an apartment to rent. A recent graduate of Pratt Institute and an Army veteran, Bill Curtis wanted to move from Brooklyn to Manhattan, nearer to his work at a firm on Second Avenue. Detmold showed him an apartment in a brownstone at 221 East 48th Street, the Russel Wright house, named for the designer who had transformed the old building into a contemporary space in the 1940s. Bill Curtis took the apartment. But Detmold was more interested in Bill for his profession than as a real estate customer. For months, Detmold had wanted to start a community newsletter, and had been looking for a graphics specialist to help him. Before long, the first issue of the *Turtle Bay Gazette* was in the mail, and Bill Curtis had begun what was to become a decades-long commitment to the neighborhood.

Detmold was soon named president of the Turtle Bay Association, working alongside Amster, who remained chairman. Detmold also served on the Community Planning Board* and spearheaded an alliance of East Side residential groups, called the East Side Residential Association. He frequently made trips to Albany to lobby for legislation, and he was well known around City Hall.

In 1967, in his role as head of the Turtle Bay Association, Detmold was named to an advisory group to begin planning expansion of United Nations–related facilities in the area. "We have been asked to assist in the planning to bring true local community participation into this initial phase," he said.

Over the next four years, the planning effort would take many unexpected turns. Changing architectural designs would turn advocates into adversaries in a struggle between the needs of the United Nations and the Turtle Bay residential community surrounding it.

THE U.N. EXPANDS: FOUR PLANS

By 1966, just 15 years after the United Nations first moved into its Turtle Bay headquarters, its member nations had more than doubled, from 60 to 122. The number of organizations related to the United Nations had grown almost as much, and an average of 6,000 tourists visited the U.N. complex each day.

The United Nations was fast outgrowing the space in its riverfront headquarters buildings. Already, two agencies—the United Nations Development Program and United Nations Children's Fund—had been forced to rent space in other locations. And the growing corps of diplomats and visiting dignitaries needed more nearby hotel space, restaurants, housing, schools, and recreation facilities.

---

* Manhattan's 12 Community Boards (originally called Community Planning Boards) are made up of volunteers appointed by the Manhattan borough president to represent the community's interests in various matters including development, planning, and land use.

That year, a group called the East River–Turtle Bay Fund, with grants from the Ford Foundation and the Rockefeller Brothers Fund, began to study how and where more space could be provided for the United Nations. The group had the full support of Mayor Lindsay. "The Mayor recognized the contribution the U.N. makes to the city," says Donald Elliott, then counsel to Lindsay and later chairman of the City Planning Commission, "It was clear to us that as the U.N.'s host city, we had an obligation to help them with their office and housing needs, and to do so within the immediate vicinity of the United Nations."

The fund's preliminary planning focused on properties directly south of the United Nations. Envisioned among a series of plans was an office building on a U-shaped plot of land owned by the city that surrounded the Queens-Midtown Tunnel ventilating shaft at the southeast corner of First Avenue and 42nd Street.*

Soon, the group was formalized under the name Fund for Area Planning and Development. Now working with the highly regarded architectural firm of Kevin Roche John Dinkeloo and Associates—and with an advisory council of city and U.N. officials and community leaders, including Peter Detmold—the planning got more specific.

On April 11, 1968, Governor Nelson Rockefeller and Mayor Lindsay announced the group's dramatic plan, the sheer magnitude of which surprised many neighbors.

The properties south of 42nd Street no longer were the focus. Instead, at the heart of the proposal was a "super block" to be created by closing and eliminating 44th Street between First and Second Avenues. Twin 44-story towers and four lower-rise buildings would provide office,

---

* The city had acquired the land when the tunnel project was started in 1937 and converted it to public parkland. In 1981, the City Council passed legislation to name it Robert Moses Playground.

hotel, and residential space, all amidst a setting of grassy parkland. In addition, First Avenue would be closed to through automobile traffic from 42nd to 47th Street, and would become a visitors' observation area surrounded by landscaping of trees and shrubs. Finally, a walkway above street level would connect the super block with Dag Hammarskjold Plaza, a narrow strip of parkland at 47th Street that was slated for improvements. When complete, a pedestrian would be able to walk from the center of Dag Hammarskjold Plaza all the way to Tudor City, a 12-building housing complex south of 43rd Street, without ever having to cross a city street.

Detmold strongly supported the design. "It will enhance our residential community," he told neighbors.

Not everyone saw it that way. To make way for the super block, land had to be cleared between First and Second Avenues. Much of it was warehouses, loft buildings, and garages, but it also included some small apartment buildings and the two large Beaux-Arts Apartments at 307 and 310 East 44th Street, built by Raymond Hood and Kenneth Murchison in 1930. Some 600 households would be displaced. Also to be torn down were two First Avenue office buildings just recently completed: the Church Peace Center and the national headquarters of the Boys Clubs of America. "I wish someone had told us about this before," the Church Center's director said at the time. Tudor City residents, living just south of the proposed super block, feared their buildings, too, might be swept up in the expansion.

But the plan moved ahead. On May 31, 1968, Governor Rockefeller signed legislation to create an entity called the United Nations Development Corporation (UNDC), which would have the authority to implement the expansion. Under UNDC's charter, it would finance, build, and operate the buildings using private financing through the issuance of bonds. UNDC also took over the planning activities, continuing to work with architect Kevin Roche.

The plan needed approval at several levels, including the Board of Estimate's go-ahead. Mayor Lindsay and Governor Rockefeller said they would consult with citizens' groups about relocation concerns. But opposition was clearly building. There was talk from some city groups of trying to repeal the May legislation.

Soon, the United Nations announced plans for a three-acre park esplanade along the East River waterfront and a seven-story office building on the parkland next to the tunnel ventilating tower at 42nd Street and First Avenue, a concept similar to the initial 1966 plan. While separate from the UNDC's proposal, the esplanade and office building were intended to complement UNDC's massive super block of towers and green space.*

By November 1969, the project design and scope had changed for the third time. It was larger still. The super block with its two tall buildings and abundant green space had given way to an enormous complex of four 40-story towers virtually enclosed by reflecting glass. "Radical," the *New York Times* called it.

Gone was the park-like feel of the earlier plan that appealed to Peter Detmold. Gone, too, was the observation area and greenery covering First Avenue. Saved were the Church Peace Center and the Boys Clubs headquarters, the two new buildings on First Avenue. But what remained in the new plan was colossal. Still a super block that would eliminate 44th Street between First and Second Avenues, it called for 4.2 million square feet of space in the four 40-story towers stretching from 43rd to 45th Street. The towers would be enclosed in a glass structure that itself would be 40 stories high. (Architecture critic Ada

---

* The U.N.'s esplanade/building plan never moved forward, after it failed to get Congressional approval for a U.S. contribution of $20 million.

Louise Huxtable noted that St. Peter's dome could fit comfortably inside.) At the base of the complex would be a park, enclosed within the massive glass bubble. "This will provide the neighborhood with much needed public open space," the UNDC's project brochure said. But to Turtle Bay neighbors, the interior public space was a poor substitute for the outdoor grassy areas they had welcomed in the previous plan.

The project's cost was $300 million, to be financed though the issuance of UNDC bonds. In square feet, it was one-third larger than the previous plan because, UNDC officials explained, more commercial space was needed to make it financially viable. Since the earlier plan had been announced, costs had risen and hoped-for federal money had not been forthcoming.

The proposal was in trouble from the start. It required relaxation of zoning regulations to accommodate its bulk, a variance from a floor area ratio (FAR) of 10 to 18, which would have been the highest in the city to date. Residents were concerned about congestion, both vehicular and pedestrian, as a result of four 40-story buildings rising on such a small area, and they feared that granting a zoning change for one project would only encourage others to ask for similar variances.

Publicly criticizing the plan were Congressman Ed Koch, who represented Turtle Bay in Washington, and City Councilmembers Carol Greitzer and Carter Burden, who charged that the community had been left out of the planning. At the City Planning Commission's first hearing on the matter in December 1969, Detmold, too, attacked the new approach, saying, "Not since Manhattan Island was stolen from the Indians for $24 in junk jewelry has such a barefaced real estate swindle been attempted in New York City."

Other community groups joined the protest. And the area's state assemblyman, Andrew Stein, was among a vocal group who called for the whole project to be moved to Welfare Island (now Roosevelt Island).

In the end, the super block was never realized. Through a combination of community opposition, politics, and financial problems, the project was scaled back considerably. In June 1971, more than five years after the initial planning began, UNDC announced a compromise project. One building, 39 stories tall—the same height as the U.N. Secretariat Building—would be built at the corner of 44th Street and First Avenue. It would house offices and a hotel. Community groups welcomed it.

On Thursday, November 20, 1975, Mayor Abraham Beame joined U.N. Secretary General Kurt Waldheim and New York Senator Daniel Patrick Moynihan at the corner of 44th Street and First Avenue to formally open One United Nations Plaza. A glass tower of office space and a 292-room hotel, the building had been financed with bonds issued by the UNDC. In the end, the state had helped secure the $55.2 million offering with a reserve fund that could be used if needed. But it was not, and the UNDC went on to finance two other buildings nearby. Two United Nations Plaza, a 40-story sister building directly next door on 44th Street, was completed in 1983; and Three United Nations Plaza, a 13-story building across the street, opened in 1987. Both housed offices and apartments for U.N. personnel.

Architecturally, the three buildings—all designed by Kevin Roche—were highly praised. Critic Paul Goldberger called Nos. One and Two, with their reflective blue-green glass wrapping towers of sloping setbacks, "exquisite minimalist sculpture." Three United Nations Plaza, with alternating bands of light and dark brown granite, was distinctly different in style from Nos. One and Two. Roche designed it to complement the glass and brick bands of the two 1930 Beaux-Arts apartment buildings down the street. Ironically, these were the same buildings that had been slated to be demolished in Roche's earlier super block plan. Now they took on renewed prominence, and in 1989 they were designated New York City landmarks.

While the three new UNDC buildings eased the office, hotel, and housing requirements at the time, U.N. expansion needs would be a recurring and controversial issue within the Turtle Bay community for many years to come.

BEEKMAN PLACE AND A BRIDGE NOT TO BE

Beekman Place is a special part of Turtle Bay. The peaceful enclave overlooking the East River from 49th Street to 51st Street—on what had been the hills of the old Beekman Farm of colonial days—has some of the most distinguished buildings in Manhattan. Its residents have always been among the city's most illustrious. Film star Myrna Loy, producer Billy Rose, and architect I. M. Pei, as well as Irving Berlin, have all lived there. And One Beekman Place, a luxury apartment building built in 1929 at the southern end of the street, was known from the beginning as home to some of the wealthiest New Yorkers. At one time, when both John D. Rockefeller III and his sister Abby "Babs" Rockefeller were living there, neighbors took to calling it simply "the Rockefeller Building."

Not surprisingly, Beekman Place residents guard their privacy. And so when it was proposed in 1958 that a bridge be built extending the southern end of Beekman across 49th Street, residents rebelled. The owner of a parking lot between 48th and 49th Streets, just north of the United Nations Gardens, was hoping to sell his land to developers for a high-rise apartment complex. In order to provide better access, he wanted city permission to build a bridge so that traffic coming from the west could use East 50th Street, turn south on Beekman and onto a ramp-like bridge that would stretch over the existing 15-foot retaining wall, to the entrance of the new apartments.

It didn't happen. Some four months after the City Planning Commission first held a hearing on the matter, the proposal was withdrawn amidst a furor from the Beekman community and the commission's finding that it would serve a private, not a public purpose.

Beekman Place was spared its bridge, and the parking lot remained— for a while. The Turtle Bay Association (at that time, still known as the East 49th Street Association) wanted the dusty, barren lot turned into a public park with an underground parking garage. "Is it really so ridiculous to want a single block on the East Side set aside for a park?" Peter Detmold asked in a letter to the *New York Times.*

The park proposal was widely reported in the media, but not seriously considered by the city. Instead, ground soon was broken for an apartment and office complex on the land. William Zeckendorf's Webb & Knapp development firm had assembled the entire block— the parking lot as well as a 17-story apartment building that would be vacated and torn down—to make way for the new project. Webb & Knapp teamed up with the Aluminum Company of America to build twin 32-story apartment towers, co-ops, atop a six-story base of offices. The apartments' entrance, on 49th Street, would be called 860 and 870 United Nations Plaza. The offices' entrance, on 48th Street, would be 866 United Nations Plaza. The architectural firm of Harrison & Abramovitz designed the towers in a style compatible with the United Nations, immediately to the south. (Wallace K. Harrison had chaired the group that designed the U.N. complex.) The modern glass building, with its floor-to-ceiling windows and spacious rooms, was unusual for a residential building in New York, and when it opened, in 1966, it attracted the elite of New York from the start.

Comedian Johnny Carson, Senator Robert Kennedy, Truman Capote, former Attorney General William Rogers (later secretary of state), *Washington Post* publisher Katharine Graham, fashion designer Bonnie Cashin, and television's David Susskind all became neighbors in the new 860–870 United Nations Plaza.

In 1967, shortly after they'd moved in, the powerful and influential residents of 860–870 did something one of them said was very "un–New York" for a Manhattan apartment building: They held a block party to get to know each other. This was not an ordinary block party. It was organized by Johnny Carson's wife, Joanne; the Susskinds helped with the invitations; a small orchestra played; and bouquets of daisies, instead of signs, led the residents to the restaurant where it was held—a place called "Inn on the Clock" on the ground floor of the building's south side. Almost everyone living in the towers came to the party. Carson even taped his *Tonight* show a half-hour early to get home in time. Mayor Lindsay dropped in to say hello, and society writer Charlotte Curtis covered the party for the *Times*. "A great building doesn't have to be dull," David Susskind told her.

Meanwhile, the sizable park Peter Detmold and his Turtle Bay associates had hoped for was not to be. But a small parcel of land on the east side of the apartment towers was converted to city parkland. Along with a block-long street that runs beside it, the park was named in 1965 for World War II hero General Douglas MacArthur. It became a children's playground called Douglas MacArthur Park. The centerpiece of the small one-third-acre park is a large concrete turtle installed by the Turtle Bay Association in the late 1990s, with an Exxon Corporation grant.

Recognizing Change

For Turtle Bay residents, the decade of the 1960s marked a time of recognition. The community had come to fully realize the challenge of living in the heart of a booming city, no longer bordered by the sheltering Third Avenue El to the west and now bounded by an expanding United Nations to the east. The community's voice had been heard throughout the city. Now, as it entered the 1970s, it faced a decade that would prove far more trying.

3. TRYING TIMES: THE 1970s

Peter's life almost hourly was fought to keep the barbarians out of the inner city.

—Julian Bach Jr., Turtle Bay neighbor, in a tribute to community leader Peter Detmold.

COMMUNITY CHALLENGED

The evening of Thursday, January 6, 1972, was cold and damp. "And it seemed particularly dark," Jeannie Sakol recalls. She and Peter Detmold and Bill Curtis joined a group of Turtle Bay Association volunteers at an apartment in the East 50s to discuss upcoming stories for the *Turtle Bay Gazette*. As was customary in the early 1970s, with the city's crime rate on the rise, they walked home together when they left the meeting shortly after 8:00 p.m. Curtis walked with Detmold and Sakol as far as the corner of 49th Street and Third Avenue. Then he headed to his apartment in the middle of the block between Second and Third. Detmold and Sakol continued on to her apartment building on the south side of 48th Street east of Third. There, under the building's awning and out of the mist, they talked for a few minutes. Then Detmold walked directly across the street to his home, an apartment he rented on the fifth floor of one of the Turtle Bay Gardens town houses, 229 East 48th Street.

At about 2:00 in the morning, Bill Curtis's telephone rang. It was the 17th Police Precinct calling. Barely able to comprehend what he heard, he turned to his wife, Colleen. "Peter Detmold's been killed."

According to police reports, the 48-year-old Detmold was stabbed as he entered his five-story walk-up building. He struggled to reach his top-floor apartment, but collapsed on the stairwell, where a neighbor found him. He was pronounced dead on arrival at Bellevue Hospital.

"A most awful, total silence" was how Jimmy Amster reflected the community's stunned reaction to Detmold's death. "We haven't even been able to grasp how enormous the gap and our loss," he said.

On January 24, more than 600 friends, family, neighbors, and city officials gathered at Holy Family Church on East 47th Street to remember Peter Detmold. Among them were Manhattan Borough President Percy Sutton, Congressman Ed Koch, Councilmembers Carol Greitzer and Carter Burden, and Assemblyman Andrew Stein.

The mourners pledged to carry on his fight. "Peter led our entire community, devoting his time and effort unstintingly and courageously to the welfare of all of us—not only in Turtle Bay but in much of Manhattan as well," said Archibald King Jr., a neighbor and fellow–Turtle Bay Association board member. "Peter's life almost hourly was fought to keep the barbarians out of the inner city," Julian Bach Jr., a neighbor and community activist, told the mourners. Borough President Sutton paid tribute to the man who he said "fought against the wave of real estate speculation that threatens to destroy the quality of life in Manhattan."

Detmold, divorced from his wife, left three daughters—15-year-old Susan and 14-year-old twins, Ellen and Jennifer. They attended the service, as did Detmold's brothers, George and John.

Neighbors and friends offered a $3,000 reward for information leading to the arrest of Detmold's murderer, and a special confidential telephone number was set up for leads to the killer. But leads were slow to come, and despite circulation of a police sketch of a suspect several weeks after the stabbing, the murder remained unsolved.

"Our greatest tribute is an absolute binding together to take over and expand the concerns, the work, the ideals of Peter in the complex job of, simply, making Manhattan a better place to live," Amster told TBA members some weeks after the murder. "From that moment of no sound [following Detmold's death], there has exploded a tremendous human clatter," he wrote. "It is the miracle of his life that the clatter is growing stronger and more and more people are joining in."

Archibald King served as interim president of the TBA immediately following Detmold's death. Shortly thereafter, Bill Curtis was elected president. Jimmy Amster remained chairman. Curtis also was appointed to Community Board 6.

Turtle Bay's Pentagon Papers

Not long after Peter Detmold died, Turtle Bay faced what many believed was its biggest challenge yet. The Metropolitan Transportation Authority (MTA) was threatening to build a huge railroad station near the community's very heart.

The passenger terminal was part of a massive $2.9 billion metropolitan-area transit plan that called for an expanded subway system and improved service on regional commuter lines, including the Long Island Rail Road (LIRR). The plan was first announced in 1968 by Governor Rockefeller and William J. Ronan, the soon-to-be chairman of the Metropolitan Transportation Authority. Then, for several years, little more was heard of it.

In November 1972, as a prerequisite for federal funding, the MTA announced a public hearing on the plan. Amster attended and came back with the news: It included a huge passenger terminal linking the LIRR to Manhattan's East Side. Another link would continue on to Kennedy International Airport. The proposed location—the northwest corner of Third Avenue and 48th Street—brought a fierce reaction from the Turtle Bay community.

"An unconscionable attempt to destroy the residential character of Turtle Bay," remarked Erik Stapper, a member of Community Board 6 and the Turtle Bay Association Board of Directors.

Stapper was an international tax attorney who lived on East 50th Street. He joined TBA President Bill Curtis in leading the community's opposition. They argued that there was no need for a new terminal anywhere in Manhattan to handle the LIRR access to the East Side. Grand Central Terminal, so close by and already an established railway station, could be used instead, they argued.

"A total waste of taxpayer money by duplicating Grand Central Terminal's under-utilized and existing facilities just a few blocks away," Stapper protested.

Hundreds of Turtle Bay residents rallied behind the opposition, with meetings, brochures, and a public relations campaign. Curtis spent mornings at Grand Central Terminal with a counter and camera,

Continued on page 97

TURTLE BAY TODAY
SIGNIFICANT BUILDINGS, LANDMARKS, AND PARKS

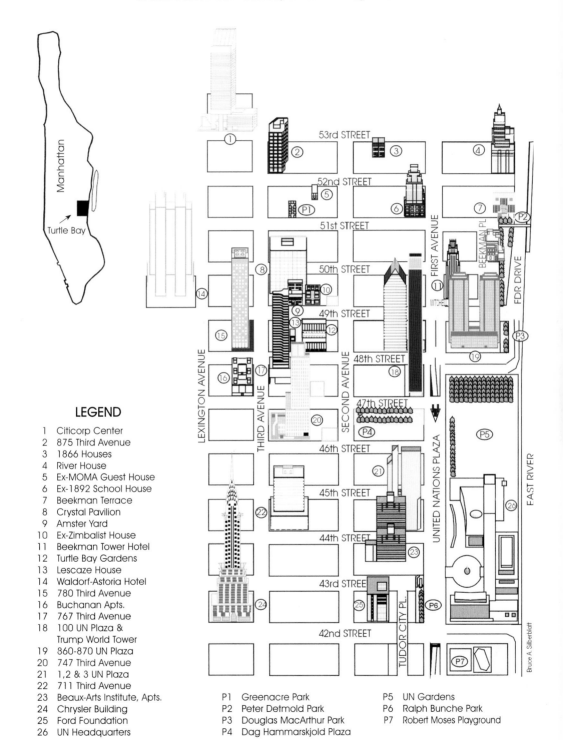

LEGEND

1 Citicorp Center
2 875 Third Avenue
3 1866 Houses
4 River House
5 Ex-MOMA Guest House
6 Ex-1892 School House
7 Beekman Terrace
8 Crystal Pavilion
9 Amster Yard
10 Ex-Zimbalist House
11 Beekman Tower Hotel
12 Turtle Bay Gardens
13 Lescaze House
14 Waldorf-Astoria Hotel
15 780 Third Avenue
16 Buchanan Apts.
17 767 Third Avenue
18 100 UN Plaza &
   Trump World Tower
19 860-870 UN Plaza
20 747 Third Avenue
21 1,2 & 3 UN Plaza
22 711 Third Avenue
23 Beaux-Arts Institute, Apts.
24 Chrysler Building
25 Ford Foundation
26 UN Headquarters

P1 Greenacre Park
P2 Peter Detmold Park
P3 Douglas MacArthur Park
P4 Dag Hammarskjold Plaza

P5 UN Gardens
P6 Ralph Bunche Park
P7 Robert Moses Playground

Bruce A. Silberblatt

65

Turtle Bay in 1853, looking north toward the higher land on which the large Beekman house, "Mount Pleasant," stood. The side of the house is seen here. This lithograph, from a drawing by B. J. Lossing, appeared in Valentine's Manual *in 1858. Later in the century, the Bay—which ran from approximately 45th Street to 48th Street—was filled in. (Collection of The New-York Historical Society; Phyllis Lucas Gallery and Old Print Center.)*

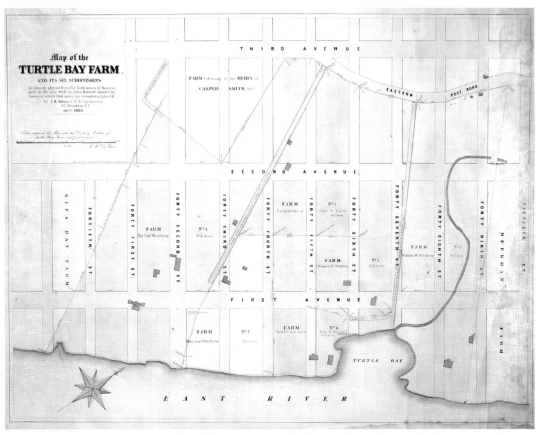

Map showing the original Turtle Bay Farm, with the city's planned straight-line street grid superimposed on it. Approved in 1811, the grid was not built in Midtown Manhattan until the middle of the century. The two diagonal lanes in the center lead to the Eastern Post Road. Turtle Creek runs into Turtle Bay, at bottom. The map was produced in 1864 from field notes of John Randel, city surveyor for the grid plan. (Collection of The New-York Historical Society.)

James Beekman's house, Mount Pleasant, with the East River in the background. During the Revolutionary War, Mount Pleasant—located at what is now the intersection of First Avenue and 51st Street—was taken over as a command post by the British, and the American patriot Nathan Hale was tried and sentenced to death there. This lithograph appeared in Valentine's Manual *in 1861. (Collection of The New-York Historical Society; Phyllis Lucas Gallery and Old Print Center.)*

First Avenue in 1946, looking south at approximately 46th Street. Tudor City can be seen on the right, with the smokestacks of the Con Edison Waterside power plant in the background. (Collection of The New-York Historical Society.)

A similar view of First Avenue less than 10 years later, shortly after the United Nations moved into its new quarters in the early 1950s. (Courtesy the United Nations.)

A south-facing view of the stockyards and breweries along the East River waterfront in 1946, as demolition was beginning, eventually making way for the United Nations. In the background, Tudor City can be seen to the right of First Avenue, and the Con Edison smokestacks at center. (Courtesy the United Nations.)

A similar view in 2007 included the U.N. Secretariat, General Assembly, and U.N. Gardens. Note Tudor City, now overshadowed by the taller Corinthian Apartments in the background. The Con Edison smokestacks are gone and the nine-acre power plant site surrounding them awaited new development.

A view of Turtle Bay in 1949, looking north from 42nd Street as construction of the Secretariat, first structure to be built on the U.N. site, gets under way. The Beekman Tower Hotel appears to the left of the construction cranes, and No. 2 and No. 1 Beekman Place are to the right. River House stands tall behind them. (Courtesy the United Nations.)

The corner of Third Avenue and 46th Street (above) looking north in the 1950s, shortly before the El stopped operating. Joe and Rose Restaurant, the canopy at right, was one of the last Third Avenue restaurants to remain open in its original location in the post-El era. First opened in 1915, it continued to welcome diners even after a high-rise office tower was built around it in the 1970s. (Photo by Lothar Stelter, © Stelterfoto LLC.) At left, decades later, Third Avenue is lined with office buildings such as Nos. 777 and 767, built by the William Kaufman Organization, considered pioneers of the avenue's early development. (Courtesy the Kaufman Organization.)

Under the stairway to the Third Avenue El's 47th Street station across from the Buchanan Apartments, in the early 1950s. The Buchanan, opened in 1928, was one of many large residential buildings constructed in Turtle Bay in the late 1920s and early 1930s. (Lothar Stelter, © Stelterfoto LLC.)

To bid farewell to the Third Avenue El and publicize the "new" avenue, city officials rode in a procession of vintage cars along the El's entire Manhattan route on August 1, 1955. They made 22 stops along the way, this one between 49th and 50th Streets near Turtle Bay's finest restaurant, Chambord (center left), and Manny Wolf's steakhouse at the corner of 49th Street (now Smith and Wollensky). Harry Hershfield, the city's chairman of Third Avenue Day, speaks to the crowd. Two days later, El demolition began. (Museum of the City of New York.)

Final pillar of the Third Avenue El, the last of Manhattan's elevated railways, is hoisted above the crowd after being pulled from its base between 42nd and 43rd Streets. The February 16, 1956, event marked the beginning of dramatic change for the neighborhood, with the avenue finally out from under the El's shadow and noise. View is to the south, with the Daily News Building in the background. (Paul Bernius/New York Daily News.*)*

The living room of Dr. and Mrs. Walton Martin's town house in Turtle Bay Gardens in the 1950s. Mrs. Martin created the Gardens, on 48th and 49th Streets between Second and Third Avenues, in 1920 from twenty 1860s brownstones. The coffered ceiling of her living room was made from original wood fencing she found in the brownstones' backyards before she converted the back lots into an Italian-inspired central garden. Turtle Bay Gardens is a New York City landmark. (Courtesy Bronson Binger.)

A pen-and-ink drawing of the willow tree in the central garden of the Turtle Bay Gardens town houses. The tree was immortalized by writer E. B. White in his 1948 essay Here is New York. The drawing is by Mabel Detmold, manager of Turtle Bay Gardens during the 1940s and 1950s. (Courtesy John Detmold.)

This painting depicts the Turtle Bay Gardens town house owned by the mid-20th century theatrical couple Ruth Gordon and Garson Kanin. The couple commissioned the watercolor and had it turned into a card they used for correspondence. Note the four cast-iron turtles that adorn the front gate, a decorative detail on many of the Turtle Bay Gardens houses.

Ruth Gordon and Garson Kanin in the living room of their town house. This is the house to which Gordon referred in the mid-1950s when she told Britain's Queen Mother that she lived "In a house in Turtle Bay, between the Waldorf and the United Nations."

Actress Katharine Hepburn, an avid gardener in the summertime, shoveled snow in front of her 49th Street Turtle Bay Gardens town house in winter, and raked leaves in her private backyard garden in the fall. In this photo, taken in the early 1980s, the rear of other town houses can be seen across the central garden, with rising towers in the background. Hepburn moved to the house in 1932, and still owned it when she died in 2003. (Photo from The Private World of Katharine Hepburn *by John Bryson. ©1990 by John Bryson. By permission Little Brown & Company.)*

Longtime Turtle Bay resident, composer and lyricist Stephen Sondheim, in the study of his town house on East 49th Street in the 1970s. The sofa is Sondheim's favorite spot for working, and the place where he has composed most of his scores over a 50-year career. He moved to Turtle Bay in 1960, shortly before A Funny Thing Happened on the Way to the Forum *opened on Broadway, earning him the first of his seven Tony awards.*

Author Kurt Vonnegut and his wife, photographer Jill Krementz, near their Turtle Bay brownstone in 1986. The couple moved to the neighborhood in 1973 shortly before Vonnegut wrote one of his many novels, Slapstick, *much of which is set in Turtle Bay. "There are no turtles. There is no bay," he wrote in the opening pages. (Courtesy Jill Krementz, all rights reserved.)*

The original entrance to Amster Yard, which James Amster, a prominent mid-20th century interior designer, transformed from a collection of old buildings that he bought in the 1940s. The Yard was Amster's home and office for many years. (Courtesy New York School of Interior Design, Robert Moyer.)

The long section of Amster Yard's L-shaped courtyard is made to appear even longer by a visual trick, a large mirror framed as an arch and suggested to James Amster by the legendary interior decorator Elsie de Wolfe. The mirror remains in the garden today. (Courtesy New York School of Interior Design, Robert Moyer.)

James Amster, who founded the Turtle Bay Association in 1957, in his lushly planted Amster Yard in the 1970s. Today Amster Yard, a New York City landmark, serves as the New York home of Spain's cultural organization, Instituto Cervantes. The courtyard, with the original iron grillwork shown here, is open to the public. (Courtesy New York School of Interior Design, Robert Moyer.)

Peter Detmold, a Turtle Bay community leader in the 1960s, was the president of the Turtle Bay Association at the time of his death in 1972 at the age of 48. This 1969 photo was taken in Detmold's 49th Street real estate office, where his business specialized in East Midtown brownstones. (Evelyn Straus/New York Daily News.)

To promote a Turtle Bay Association fundraiser to be held in the garden of the Turtle Bay Gardens town houses in 1968, TBA leaders James Amster (left) and Peter Detmold posed for this photo with the event's chairwomen, Judith Flynn (left), and Audrey Griffin. The photo was taken near the center of the garden, shared by the owners of the 20 Turtle Bay Gardens houses. The fountain is a replica of that found at Rome's Villa Medici. (Courtesy Turtle Bay Association/New York Times.)

In the early 1950s, the footbridge that connects Beekman Place to a riverside esplanade crossed over a barren strip of neglected parkland that had been created when the East River Drive was constructed in the late 1930s. (Collection of The New-York Historical Society.)

Today, the parkland—named Peter Detmold Park in 1972 and later renovated—is lushly planted, the foliage of its large trees reaching up and over the bridge itself.

In 1970, this fountain started spewing water high into the air from the southern tip of Welfare Island (now Roosevelt Island). A gift from philanthropist George Delacorte, some called it "Delacorte's Folly" when, among other mishaps, its chlorinated water blew onto Turtle Bay during high winds. It was shut down in 1986. In the background, the U.N. General Assembly (at left) and Chrysler Building (center) are visible. (AP/Wide World Photos)

Scenes from many movies have been filmed in Turtle Bay over the years, but perhaps none attracted as much attention as this scene from the 1955 movie The Seven Year Itch. *Shot late at night at the corner of 52nd Street and Lexington Avenue, Marilyn Monroe's pose over a breezy subway grate, with co-star Tom Ewell, attracted some 2,000 neighbors and paparazzi. (Courtesy Photofest.)*

Director Sydney Pollack and actor Sean Penn (left) on First Avenue in front of the U.N. in a scene from The Interpreter, *one of the most recent movies made in Turtle Bay. The suspense thriller was filmed over 15 weekends in 2004, when Penn and co-star Nicole Kidman became welcome "workers" in the neighborhood. Many Turtle Bay residents served as extras in the film. (Richard Corkery/New York* Daily News.)

Beekman Place, looking south from 51st Street, in the early 1950s. Aside from newer model cars and larger trees along its sidewalks, Beekman Place has managed to retain its quiet charm, due largely to a move by the neighborhood in the 1980s to downzone the area so that taller buildings could not be constructed there. Today, Beekman Place remains one of New York City's most coveted residential addresses. (Collection of The New-York Historical Society.)

When Greenacre Park on East 51st Street opened in 1971 (above), Turtle Bay was host to all six Rockefeller siblings, a rare public appearance together. The park was a gift from Mrs. Jean Mauze, the former Abby "Babs" Rockefeller and Beekman Place resident. From left are her brothers David, seated; Winthrop and Governor Nelson Rockefeller; William Paley; and brothers Laurance S. and John D. Rockefeller III. Parks Commissioner August Heckscher is at right. (Larry Morris/The New York Times/Redux.) Below, the park today.

Turtle Bay neighbors were wearing these green buttons in the early 1970s as part of a successful campaign to stop the Metropolitan Transportation Authority from building a passenger rail terminal at Third Avenue and 48th Street. The community won its fight when it was decided to have the rail line, a Long Island Railroad link, use the existing Grand Central Terminal instead. (Courtesy Turtle Bay Association.)

The community celebrated a victory on the steps of City Hall in October 1987, when the Board of Estimate approved a new zoning designation for much of Turtle Bay. The zoning limited the height of new mid-block construction. The move was spearheaded by the East Side Rezoning Alliance. (Courtesy Turtle Bay Association.)

The renovated Peter Detmold Park was dedicated in 1987. On hand to cut the ribbon were (from left) Community Board 6 Parks Chairman Gary Papush, TBA President Bill Curtis, City Councilwoman Carol Greitzer, City Parks Commissioner Henry Stern, City Comptroller Harrison Goldin, and City Councilman Robert Dryfoos. The park was initially named for Peter Detmold in 1972, shortly after his death. (Courtesy Turtle Bay Association.)

On the steps of City Hall in 1992, East Midtown residents protested closure of the 48th Street northbound ramp to the FDR Drive, which caused noisy, dangerous traffic tie-ups on First Avenue. Flanked by City Council members Charles Millard and Carolyn Maloney, TBA board member Bruce Silberblatt, who led the Turtle Bay community's fight, addresses the media. Closed for more than a decade, the ramp reopened in 1998. (Courtesy Turtle Bay Association.)

Ground was broken on October 12, 1994, for the long-planned renovation of Dag Hammarskjold Plaza, a strip of land that had been a neighborhood eyesore for years. Helping in the ceremony were (from left) Assemblyman John Ravitz, Congresswoman Carolyn Maloney, Friends of Dag Hammarskjold Plaza President Anne Saxon-Hersh, City Councilman Andrew Eristoff, City Parks Commissioner Henry Stern, Community Board 6 Chairman Lou Sepersky, and TBA President Bill Curtis. (Courtesy Turtle Bay Association.)

Celebrity friends and neighbors of Katharine Hepburn gathered on the actress's 90th birthday—May 12, 1997—to dedicate the Katharine Hepburn Garden in Dag Hammarskjold Plaza. On hand as Parks Commissioner Henry Stern (left) unveiled the garden's plaque were (from left, on the right side of the plaque) film director Anthony Harvey, Congresswoman Carolyn Maloney, Manhattan Borough President Virginia Fields, playwright Garson Kanin, and actresses Marian Seldes and Julie Harris. (Courtesy Turtle Bay Association.)

Author Kurt Vonnegut, a longtime Turtle Bay resident, told neighborhood stories at a Turtle Bay Association event at the corner of 49th Street and Second Avenue on a chilly March day in 2005. The occasion was the naming of the 49th Street block between Second and Third Avenues Katharine Hepburn Place, in honor of the actress who lived in Turtle Bay for more than 60 years. In the background is Bill Curtis, TBA president. (Corey Sipkin/ New York Daily News.)

The Turtle Bay Gardens town houses (the 48th Street side shown above) represent some of the best examples of the residential character Turtle Bay neighbors try to preserve. Along with Amster Yard (at left), Turtle Bay Gardens was named a New York City landmark in 1966, among the very earliest sites to be granted landmark status after enactment of the city's Landmarks Preservation Commission Law. Turtle Bay Gardens is also on the National Register of Historic Places. Today, Amster Yard is the New York home of Instituto Cervantes.

Designated a New York City landmark in 1998, the former Panhellenic Tower, by John Mead Howells, was built in 1928 as a women's hotel and later converted to today's Beekman Tower Hotel. It is located at the northeast corner of 49th Street and First Avenue.

Modernist architect William Lescaze, designer of many Turtle Bay buildings, converted a 19th-century brownstone into a modern town house for his home and office in 1934. The house, on 48th Street between Second and Third Avenues, was named a city landmark in 1976.

The former Rockefeller/Museum of Modern Art Guest House, created from a carriage house by architect Philip Johnson in 1950, originally served as a house for guests of the Rockefeller brothers, and later for museum guests. Located on East 52nd Street, it was given city landmark status in 2000.

These two clapboard houses, located at 312–314 East 53rd Street, were built in 1866, shortly before frame houses in the area were outlawed as a fire threat. The house at right was designated a New York City landmark in 1968, the one at left in 2000.

At left, the 1928 Beaux-Arts Institute of Design, by Frederick Hirons, was given city landmark status in 1988. At right, the 1930s Beaux-Arts Apartments, by Raymond Hood and Kenneth Murchison, were landmarked the next year. Both are located on 44th Street between First and Second Avenues. (Courtesy Debra Pickrel.)

The Efrem Zimbalist House, at 225–227 East 49th Street, dates from 1928 and was the home of violinist Efrem Zimbalist and his wife, opera singer Alma Gluck, for many years. In 1957, the 20-room mansion became a temporary station house for the 17th Police Precinct. The police officers' presence there indirectly helped neighbors stop the city from widening two of the area's crosstown streets. Today, the old mansion houses apartments.

Built in 1892, former Public School 135 today serves as the façade for a 20-story apartment building. Located at the northwest corner of First Avenue and 51st Street, the school was threatened with demolition in the 1980s, when neighbors banded together to preserve it. The school house is listed on the National Register of Historic Places.

Since it opened in 1999, the new Dag Hammarskjold Plaza has become Turtle Bay's "Central Park" for neighborhood residents and "Gateway to the United Nations" for all.

tally up peak-hour passenger traffic to demonstrate that the old terminal had under-utilized capacity.

Before long, Turtle Bay neighbors were wearing big green "Terminate the Terminal" buttons on their lapels. And they started referring to the site of the proposed terminal as "One Ronan Plaza," a reference to the MTA chairman.

In late February 1973, the TBA announced that Congressman Koch would attend a public meeting to address the threat. Flyers, bulletins, and posters blanketed the community. "It would have been hard to be in Turtle Bay and not know about the meeting," Stapper says today.

Indeed, an important anonymous "someone" did get the message. Shortly before the meeting at the Holy Family Church auditorium on East 47th Street, an envelope was delivered to the TBA office. "Its contents were truly astonishing," Stapper says.

It contained a copy of a report prepared for the MTA by a big consulting engineering firm, Parson Brinckerhoff Quade and Douglas. It concluded that the Third Avenue location was so poor a choice for a LIRR terminal as to not warrant further study. And it went on to outline the technical reasons to bring the LIRR link into Grand Central instead.

"It was just what we had been saying," says Stapper, "and now we had a report by the MTA's own consultants with the same opinion. We were stunned."

But more astounding to Stapper was the date of the report— January 29, 1968, a month before Governor Rockefeller and Ronan originally announced the new transit plan. "It was now clear that the MTA had totally ignored its own experts' advice from Day One," he says.

The report's disclosure boosted the TBA campaign. The Koch meeting drew a standing-room-only crowd, and a few weeks later at another gathering, more than 750 neighbors heard from a host of local elected officials who supported Turtle Bay's position.

Still, the MTA didn't back down. The project went before the Federal Urban Mass Transportation Administration in Washington, awaiting approval of the U.S. government's share of the funding. The federal agency said it would look at the Grand Central alternative.

Meanwhile, Curtis and Stapper prepared a 28-page critique of the plan that the TBA sent to Governor Rockefeller, Ronan, the Board of Estimate, and others. It urged the MTA to accept the Parsons Brinckerhoff report, the study prepared for the MTA some five years earlier.

The TBA was suddenly the center of media attention. Stapper was the subject of television, radio, and newspaper interviews. The *New York Times*, in an article on the terminal issue on July 8, 1973, called the Turtle Bay community "one of the most resourceful development fighters in the city."

The tide had turned, although it would be four more years before the location of the LIRR access to the East Side would finally be determined.

In June 1977, Mayor Beame announced his support of the Grand Central Terminal location. And on July 8—almost 10 years after the plan was first introduced—the MTA announced that the LIRR link would use Grand Central Terminal. The Third Avenue terminal was no longer an option.

"It was a huge victory for the community," says Stapper. "We felt we had fought a good fight. But Congressman Koch deserved much of the credit for sticking behind us in our struggle."

Turtle Bay neighbors who had jokingly referred to the planned terminal site as "One Ronan Plaza" now called it "Ronan's Tomb."

The identity of the anonymous person who leaked the crucial MTA report to the TBA back in 1973 was never learned. It was Turtle Bay's own "Pentagon Papers" case, Congressman Koch said at the time.

Today, a 50-story office tower stands on the site of what would have been the railroad terminal. Opened in 1983 as the Wang Building and now known simply as 780 Third Avenue, it is distinguished by its Finnish Balmoral granite construction and diagonally patterned window openings. Meanwhile, after a series of financial delays and technical studies, construction of the project to bring LIRR service into Grand Central, called East Side Access, got underway in 2001 and was scheduled for completion in 2013.

Copter Controversy

Just five months before Turtle Bay residents claimed victory for "terminating" the Third Avenue terminal, Mayor Beame was helicoptered to the top of the 59-story Pan Am Building, at Park Avenue and 45th Street, for a ceremony that, far from a victory, marked a defeat for the Turtle Bay Association. There, on January 31, 1977, he cut the ribbon to resume regularly scheduled helicopter flights from the building's rooftop heliport to New York City's three area airports.

He was not the first mayor to cut a ribbon to initiate helicopter service from the building. Eleven years earlier, then-Mayor Wagner had done the honors, with Governor Rockefeller standing by and Vice President Hubert Humphrey calling in with congratulations.

But the flights were suspended in early 1968 when the helicopter operator, financially-strapped New York Airways, could no longer afford to continue the service.

Living under the flight path of the helicopters, the Turtle Bay community had vigorously opposed the service as soon as it was first announced in the early 1960s. Residents joined businessmen and owners of the area's major office buildings in trying to stop it. Flying the 25-passenger twin-rotor aircraft over the densely populated section of Manhattan was dangerous and noisy, all agreed.

The commercial interests took the lead. They formed a coalition that included owners of the 77-story Chrysler Building and 56-story Chanin Building. But their well-financed campaign, with high-powered lawyers and public relations support, could not stop what the coalition called "obvious madness." The City Planning Commission eased zoning restrictions to pave the way for the service, and the Board of Estimate unanimously approved the start-up. Flights began on December 21, 1965.

For the next two years, Turtle Bay residents complained of the noise and constant fear of an accident overhead. "Sleepless nights of fearful slap-bang racket," one resident said.

So when New York Airways suspended its flights for financial reasons, neighbors breathed a sigh of relief.

The relief lasted nine years. And then, in August 1976, a strengthened New York Airways announced it would start up again. This time it would use a slightly larger aircraft, a 30-passenger single-rotor Sikorsky 61 that was quieter than the old choppers and had an excellent safety record, the airline said.

Residents' groups took the lead in fighting approval. "Tell us why helicopter flights can't be confined to riverfront sites," TBA President Bill Curtis asked at a City Planning Commission hearing, "A quiet Midtown residential area is no place to interject the noise and safety hazards that copters present." Murray Hill and Tudor City groups joined the protests.

Despite objections from the residential groups, the two community boards in the area—Community Boards 5 and 6—voted for it, and the City Planning Commission and Board of Estimate approved the flights in relatively quick order. Mayor Beame's ribbon-cutting ceremony in late January 1977 initiated a schedule of some 50 flights a day.

"We get an echo chamber effect from the helicopters," said H. Jeremy Wintersteen, a TBA board member. "But what can we do? At first, we fought. We lost. We're beaten."

Less than four months later, in the late afternoon of Monday, May 16, a young accountant, Anne Barnecott, was standing in line at the corner of Madison and 43rd Street, waiting for a bus to take her to her home in the Bronx. Above her, in the offices of the Pan Am Building, the airline's workers were getting ready to leave for the day. "I heard a loud thump, and the building shook just a little," says Mari Fransson, a Pan American World Airways secretary who was on the 45th floor at the time. She worried that the sound might be coming from the helipad above her.

On the roof, chaos had broken out. A Sikorsky 61's landing gear had collapsed, its rotor blades hitting the roof and breaking into parts. Four passengers about to board the flight were killed. And one of the blade sections flew over the rooftop's edge, plummeting to the street and killing Miss Barnecott as she waited for her bus.

The Turtle Bay Association's reaction was sharp. Chairman Jimmy Amster sent a telegram to Mayor Beame's office: "Your vote in favor of helicopter service to the Pan Am Building made today's tragedy possible. Urge complete re-evaluation of need for service and safety of all New Yorkers before service is reinstated."

Mayor Beame ordered an immediate shutdown of service pending a National Transportation Safety Board (NTSB) investigation.

The next month, a meeting of local community leaders was scheduled in the Pan Am Building to review the future of helicopter service in light of the horrific accident. George Hambleton, a senior executive of Pan Am and New York Airways, was to appear before the group.

When Turtle Bay neighbor Jeannie Sakol—long ago fed up with noisy rattling windows and dangerous skies over her East 48th Street apartment—heard about the meeting, she decided to make some "noise" of her own. Taking a page from high-profile New York City "baby stroller" protests of the past, she started calling neighborhood mothers. Before long, she had put together a baby-carriage brigade of moms, nannies, tots, dogs, and babies. They marched to the 45th Street entrance of the Pan Am Building on the day of the meeting. There, they got plenty of attention from a gathering crowd and Sakol, a TBA Board member, recounts today, "We were met by some very befuddled, and rude, security guards. But I never knew for sure that our message got through to the airline's higher levels."

"Oh, we heard all right," says George Hambleton today. As he was about to leave the meeting that day, he was handed a note: "Suggest not exit building through 45th Street side."

Hambleton took the advice of his aides. Sakol and the Turtle Bay moms may not have realized it at the time, but their protest had indeed had an effect. It was just one more indication to New York Airways and the city that this time, the neighborhood would not allow service to start up again. The helicopter flights were never resumed.*

Fountain Folly and Waterfall Wonder

"Crazy" was the word George Delacorte's wife used when he came up with the idea to give New York City a geyser-like fountain in the middle of the East River. It would spew water 450 feet into the air at the southern tip of Welfare Island (now Roosevelt Island) across from Turtle Bay and the United Nations. Valerie Delacorte predicted it would come to be known as "Delacorte's Folly."

But the Dell Publishing founder and philanthropist was determined. He had already financed the Alice in Wonderland sculpture in Central Park and given a musical clock with twirling animals to the park's Children's Zoo. Now, he wanted to see a fountain spectacle on the East River, patterned after Switzerland's 75-year-old *Jet d'Eau* on Lake Geneva.

The fountain had problems from the start. First, the Swiss refused to help Delacorte's architects with the design. The Swiss told him it was a "state secret," he said. When his architects finally did devise a plan, Turtle Bay residents grew concerned that high winds would blow polluted water on the neighborhood. And how could passengers on touring Circle Line boats not get drenched by the dirty water?

So a chlorination system was added to the plans. And Delacorte agreed that if the winds were more than 12 miles per hour, the fountain would be turned off.

---

* In October 1977, the NTSB determined that a metal fatigue crack in the chopper's landing gear had caused the accident.

The thin water spray was tested for more than a year before it finally started regular operations in the summer of 1970. It ran four hours each day, from noon to 2:00 p.m. and 8:00 p.m. to 10:00 p.m. At night, it was illuminated by eight floodlights, creating such an eye-catching sight that rubber-necking motorists backed up on the Franklin Delano Roosevelt (FDR) Drive. Then area residents complained that trees were dying on Welfare Island, the result of the chlorinated water. Some criticized Delacorte's whimsical expense at a time when the city appeared headed toward a serious fiscal crisis. And finally, when plans for a huge Roosevelt Island housing development were announced, there was talk of having to relocate or remove the fountain altogether.

But it sputtered along, off and on, until 1986, when it finally broke down and was quietly shut off for good. By then, most of the neighborhood was referring to the fountain as "Delacorte's Folly."

About the same time Delacorte's ill-fated fountain started gushing out chlorinated water in 1970, a more traditional water work was taking shape in Turtle Bay. This would be a 25-foot-high waterfall over a wall of sculpted granite, the centerpiece of a tiny landscaped "pocket park" being built on East 51st Street.

The green haven was a gift of Mrs. Jean Mauze, the former Abby "Babs" Rockefeller, youngest of John D. Rockefeller Jr.'s six children and a longtime Beekman Place resident. Mauze had purchased three lots on the north side of 51st Street between Second and Third Avenues. There she asked landscape architect Hideo Sasaki to design a park where she said she hoped neighbors would "find some moments of serenity in this busy world."

Sasaki designed the 60-foot-wide park on three levels, with a mass of falling water at the lower level, a trickling brook and trellis roof over tables and chairs surrounded by honey locust trees, bright masses of rhododendron and azalea, and pots of seasonal flowers. Mauze called it Greenacre Park.

The park's opening on October 14, 1971 was notable not only because of Greenacre's idyllic beauty, but also because all five of Mauze's illustrious brothers came to the ceremony. It was rare that all the Rockefeller children gathered together publicly. But joining their sister in Turtle Bay that day were John D. III, Laurance, David, Winthrop, and Nelson, then New York's governor.

Mauze had lived in Turtle Bay since 1930. Her first husband, investment banker David M. Milton, led the syndicate that built the luxurious 19-story co-op apartment building One Beekman Place in 1929. When it was completed, "Babs" and her husband moved into one of its 24 spacious apartments, an 18-room triplex facing the East River. Her brother John D. Rockefeller III, who helped finance the building, moved into another. Mauze lived at One Beekman until her death in 1976 at the age of 72.

Mauze's love for nature didn't stop with her pretty park. Through the years, she and her Greenacre Foundation generously contributed to Turtle Bay causes and to the Turtle Bay Tree Fund, a neighborhood organization that keeps the area green with trees, ivy, and flowers.

GREENING OF A NEIGHBORHOOD

When Edmund "Ted" Stanley moved to Beekman Place in 1973, his neighbor across the street, noted philanthropist Mary Lasker, found a kindred spirit. And Stanley found a volunteer job.

Lasker had long lived at 29 Beekman Place. Best known for her contributions to medical research through the Lasker Foundation, she was beloved throughout the city for planting trees and flowers, from her earliest tree plantings along 57th Street to her colorful tulips on Park Avenue's malls. In the early 1950s, she had donated 300 cherry trees and tens of thousands of white daffodils to the United Nations Gardens in memory of her late husband, the prominent advertising executive Albert Lasker.

But she also took a personal interest in her own street. Her gardener planted tulips in the Beekman Place tree beds each spring and chrysanthemums in the fall. And she was a major contributor to the Turtle Bay Tree Fund, which planted the summertime flowers. When Stanley learned of Lasker's role in making his new street so attractive, he wrote to thank her. He ended his note: "If ever I can help with the wonderful things you do, I hope you will let me know."

A few weeks later, Lasker wrote back: "There is a Turtle Bay Tree Fund which you could contribute to, if you wish. . . . I am so grateful to hear from someone else who is interested in the looks of our town."

Stanley wrote back: "I have now come to know the people at the Tree Fund and have made a contribution."

A year later, he wrote again: "I became a contributor, was elected a director and now I am president," he reported to Lasker.

Thus began Ted Stanley's long stint as head of the Tree Fund. The chairman of financial printer Bowne & Company, Stanley's energy and enthusiasm—and his generous financial support—helped the fund thrive and build on an effort that had begun just a few years earlier.

It was Lowell Hanson who started the Tree Fund back in the 1960s, shortly after he moved to Turtle Bay Gardens. A vice president with Continental Can Company, Hanson and his wife, Suzanne, were avid gardeners in their own backyard terrace. Soon their attention shifted to the bare tree beds on the street side of their

49th Street house, then to beds in front of their neighbors' houses and on around the corner to 48th Street. When Hanson served as president of the Turtle Bay Association, he decided to set up a separate entity, the Turtle Bay Tree Fund, to solicit contributions solely for community landscaping.

Soon tree beds were being cleaned regularly, ivy was planted, and daffodils bloomed in the spring and begonias in the summer.

Turtle Bay's beautification program was recognized throughout the city. In 1966, the TBA and the Tree Fund were cited by Mayor Lindsay "for the most outstanding contribution . . . to the beautification of New York through their tree planting in the Turtle Bay area."

When Hanson moved from New York City in the late 1960s, others carried on the program: first Budd Buszek, and then Jeannie Sakol and Prue Bach shared the responsibility until Lasker used her persuasive touch on her new neighbor, Ted Stanley. In later years, Doug Moat and Emilia Laboda led the fund and Bill Huxley was named president in 2002.*

Today, the Turtle Bay Tree Fund, which since Lasker's death in 1994 continues to receive support from her Salute to the Seasons Fund, maintains tree beds on designated cross streets throughout much of Turtle Bay and on several blocks of First Avenue. The TBA handles maintenance along Second Avenue from 43rd to 53rd Street.

HURRICANE WINDS

In 1976, New York City struggled to recover from its worst financial crisis in history. Thousands of municipal workers had been fired,

---

* Today, a bronze plaque at the northeast corner of 49th Street and First Avenue recognizes the early landscaping efforts of Lowell Hanson, who died in 1976.

others saw their wages frozen, and city services had been drastically reduced.

In August of that year, a hurricane named Belle skirted the city. Its 120-mile-per-hour winds made landfall on Long Island, but Manhattan, too, was whipped by winds of up to 60 miles per hour. The willow tree in Turtle Bay Gardens, the tree immortalized in E. B. White's writings about New York, survived the storm, but only after a remarkable coincidence. Just hours before Belle struck, one of the willow's heavy branches snapped off and fell to the ground. Gardens residents quickly summoned pruners to trim the tree's other vulnerable limbs. While smaller and less shapely for sure, the old willow withstood the storm.

Two days after the August 10 hurricane, the *New York Times* published an editorial titled "A Parable for New York," illustrated by a drawing of the willow tree, the pen-and-ink sketch Mabel Detmold had done for her little book of house biographies.

The parable began: "In a garden of Turtle Bay grows an old, much-cherished willow tree whose fate has been linked in the literature of New York to the fate of the city itself. . . ."

And it ended: "Drawing strength from an old underground stream that still flows beneath its roots, the willow will likely re-emerge next spring stronger and more luxuriant than ever. As the tree endures, so can the city—painstakingly pruned to weather its fiscal storms, but confident still."

As the decade of the 1970s ended, New York City's financial stability did begin to return. With drastically trimmed budgets, it appeared the metropolis had indeed "weathered its fiscal storms" just as the old willow had weathered the hurricane's winds. Citizens showed renewed pride in the city, businesses regained confidence in its future, and developers who had waited out the late 1970s were ready to invest in its neighborhoods once again.

On Turtle Bay's Third Avenue, where construction had slowed to a near halt in the 1970s, there would be an explosion of office building in the 1980s. But when developers started to eye Turtle Bay's quiet residential streets off the commercially zoned Third Avenue, the community would take action to forever shape the neighborhood's cityscape.

4. Sunlight Preserved: The 1980s

Sunlight and air are as important as food itself in sustaining life. They are wildly important.
—Actress Katharine Hepburn, on the need to restrict tall buildings in Turtle Bay.

Keeping the Charm

In 1984, when owners of the 36 apartments in a Venetian-style building at the north end of Beekman Place got an offer to sell it to a developer, it was déjà vu for many of them. As far back as the 1960s, the six-story Beekman Terrace, built in 1925 on a bluff overlooking the East River, had attracted the interest of big builders. City zoning regulations allowed for a high rise on the lot three times the size of Beekman Terrace, a tempting prospect for developers of the 1980s.

After a slump in the 1970s, New York City's real estate market was now booming. The residents of the Beekman Terrace co-op at 455 East 51st Street got not one, but two offers in quick succession. The higher was for $43 million.

While they mulled it over—to be accepted, two-thirds of the co-op's shares needed to be voted in favor—the potential deal served as a wake-up call to the rest of the Beekman Place community. "We recognized the superior value our street represented to developers," says Buddy Radisch, a Beekman Place resident since 1970 and a longtime Beekman Place Association president. "We were determined to preserve the quiet neighborhood character of the street."

A group of residents, headed by Andrew Blum and Radisch, formed what they called the Riverfront 50s Association to lobby the city to change the Beekman area's zoning regulations. They wanted to limit new buildings to no more than approximately five stories, the general height of town houses on the street.* While they primarily wanted to preserve the character of their quiet, secluded community, the group also pointed to safety issues. Beekman Place and the three dead-end streets leading to it are unusually narrow, a safety concern if congested streets should prohibit fire trucks from passing through.

Not everyone on Beekman Place agreed with the "downzoning" goal. The owners at One Beekman Place, the 19-story 1929 building at the street's south end, were opposed. The building had an adjacent one-story garage on its east side, and while the owners said they had no intention of selling it, they didn't want to forfeit the potential value of the garage's air rights. The owners of vacant town houses on the river side of Beekman Place, Nos. 25 and 27, also were opposed.

"Zoning at the time would have allowed for lots and air rights to be assembled so that a 40-story building could have gone up on the 25–27 site," says Radisch. "We had to stop it."

The Turtle Bay Association supported the Riverfront 50s Association, but the four-year-old Beekman Place Association, representing most of the buildings in the Beekman Place community, did not take a position because of the split among its members.

As the re-zoning proposal appeared to be moving toward approval, the Beekman Terrace negotiations broke off, at least in part because the buyer was concerned about the effect of a zoning change. The Riverfront 50s Association continued its fight. On July 16, 1985, just

---

* In New York City zoning parlance, it was a change from a high density residential R10 District to a low density R8B District.

before the Board of Estimate's final vote, a group of 350 residents of the wealthy Beekman area gathered to rally support for the plan. Two days later, they proclaimed victory as the board unanimously voted approval. Court appeals followed but none were successful.

Meanwhile, the town houses at Nos. 25–27 remained vacant for years, and then in 1997, they were sold and converted into a six-story condominium building, a move that pleased Beekman residents.

Beekman now saved, the crusade to downzone would shift to other parts of Turtle Bay.

Don't Slay Turtle Bay

"Sunlight and air are as important as food itself in sustaining life. They are wildly important!" The words of wisdom came from the actress Katharine Hepburn, delivered to a rally of her fellow Turtle Bay Association members on Thursday, May 21, 1987. The demonstrators, led by another neighbor—NBC newscaster Edwin Newman— gathered to push for approval of a proposal that would stop out-of-scale buildings from rising on Turtle Bay mid-blocks.

"I am 100 percent in favor of what the Association is doing," Hepburn said. Stephen Sondheim also sent a message of support, and another Turtle Bay neighbor, Kurt Vonnegut, held a briefing for the press. The neighborhood slogan soon became "Don't Slay Turtle Bay."

Several hundred residents joined the rally on East 52nd Street in front of five 100-year-old brownstones on the north side of the street. The five-story houses symbolized what the neighborhood was trying to stop: The owner planned to tear them down to build a 15- to 20-story residential hotel.

The move to downzone Turtle Bay had actually started several years earlier when Irene Peveri, a former resident of East 52nd Street who had moved to Murray Hill, lost the view from four of her apartment windows to a tall, narrow "sliver" building that went up immediately next door. "At that point, I had to do something," says Peveri, a member of Community Board 6 and longtime advocate of preserving the character of local neighborhoods. She formed the East Side Rezoning Alliance (ESRA) and together with Turtle Bay resident Ellen Blair, brought together some 15 East Side community groups—including the TBA, Riverfront 50s Association, Sutton Area Community, the Murray Hill Committee (later called the Murray Hill Neighborhood Association) and Community Board 6—to push for zoning changes.

With funding help from the nonprofit Greenacre Foundation, the group commissioned a study of an area that included parts of Turtle Bay: the mid-blocks between First and Second Avenues from 49th Street to 53rd Street, and between Second and Third Avenues from 48th to 53rd Street.

By the spring of 1986, ESRA presented its study and a plan to the City Planning Commission. Similar to the rezoning of the Beekman area, it called for limiting the height of mid-block buildings to the general height of the old structures around them.

For months, the plan remained at the City Planning Commission— "in a musty resting place," as one Turtle Bay neighbor put it—seemingly forgotten.

In the spring of 1987, when the brownstones on 52nd Street were threatened with imminent razing, the community's residents decided to take action. They secured 1,000 signatures on a petition calling for a halt to the developer's plans, held a press conference, solicited media interviews, and rallied at the site before television cameras and news photographers. *New York Post* gossip columnist Cindy Adams warned Mayor Koch about "tangling with the indomitable Katie Hepburn."

The *New York Times* and *Newsday* carried stories.

"In the end, they must have heard," says TBA's Bill Curtis, "because by late June, the City Planning Commission had certified the plan and it was on its way through the approval process."

It landed before the Board of Estimate for final approval on Thursday, October 29. Leaving nothing to chance, Community Board 6 Land Use Chair Brenda Levin led a busload of Turtle Bay residents to City Hall the day of the vote. More than 60 East Side neighbors signed up to speak at the board's open meeting. When Peveri rose and asked the crowd how many in the room supported the zoning change, the entire audience stood up and cheered wildly.

Just a few hours later, the Board of Estimate approved the new zoning designation for the Turtle Bay blocks, along with the blocks from East 53rd to East 59th Street between First and Second Avenues and Sutton Square, a small area east of Sutton Place between 57th and 59th Streets. "Nobody was about to slay Turtle Bay," says Curtis, who is quick to credit the East Side Rezoning Alliance for initiating the move and its persistence in assuring approval.*

Meanwhile, the five brownstones on 52nd Street did not escape bulldozing. However, thanks to the downzoning, the height of the new building that went up on the site—the Hungarian Mission to the United Nations, designed by Emery Roth & Sons—is consistent with the structures surrounding it.

A Park Named Peter Detmold

In June 1940, to mark the opening of the stretch of the East River Drive from 49th Street to 92nd Street, some 1,700 invited guests

---

* The change was generally from an R10 District to an R8B District, although residents had hoped for a somewhat less dense designation for the 48th and 49th Street blocks of Turtle Bay Gardens.

boarded two excursion steamers for a cruise along the East River waterfront. With city officials narrating, the guests were regaled with stories about construction of the modern new thoroughfare. The city was quick to point out that every available inch of land along the route had been preserved for parks or recreation areas. The most notable example was Carl Schurz Park at the north, with its promenade built over the Drive's top level. But along the Midtown stretch, too, small pockets of land had been saved for recreation areas. At 58th, 57th, and 56th Streets and also at 53rd Street—the inspiration for Sidney Kingsley's 1930s play *Dead End*—tiny park areas were set aside. And between 49th and 51st Streets, a larger—though still small—stretch of land was saved for parkland.

This one-acre triangular sliver of land was sandwiched between the Drive and Beekman Place. In the early 1940s, it was planted with trees and shrubs and connected by a footbridge to a riverside esplanade running to the north. But over the years the park became a neglected plot of land. In fact, it had no name. The first edition of the classic *AIA Guide to New York City*, published in 1967, lists it as "Unnamed Park," and City Parks Department maps of the time called it simply "park area." But Turtle Bay neighbors recognized its potential and in the early 1970s, Peter Detmold, among others, was pushing for improvements.

After Detmold's death in 1972, the first step toward upgrading the park was taken when the Turtle Bay Association and Community Board 6 urged that the park be given a proper name. City Councilmember Carol Greitzer introduced the legislation, and soon the two-block stretch of greenery along the waterfront was officially known as "Peter Detmold Park."

Repairs and some improvements were made at the time, but the city's fiscal crisis interfered with grander plans until the early 1980s. Jimmy Amster, in particular, kept pushing for a major renovation until finally, in 1984, proposals for the park's total redo were undertaken in earnest. Amster died in June 1986 at the age of 77, and never saw the park completed. But shortly before his death, he learned that a final design had been approved and funding was available. Construction would begin within months.

On October 21, 1986, Peter Detmold's twin daughters, Jennifer and Ellen, now in their late 20s, joined Greitzer, City Parks Commissioner Henry Stern, Bill Curtis, and others at a groundbreaking ceremony to mark the start of a $794,000 restoration of Peter Detmold Park. "Our father was always trying to preserve the neighborhood," Ellen Detmold remembered. She said she and her sister knew their father would have been very touched by the tribute to him.

An even bigger crowd of officials and neighbors attended the grand opening a year later. The park had undergone a complete makeover. Landscape architects Burt Blumberg and Ann Butter softened the lines of the narrow stretch of land, creating new seating areas and landscaped gardens to include 38 new trees, from Canadian hemlocks to dogwoods, along with rhododendron bushes and flowering plants.

At the ceremony, Commissioner Stern dedicated the park's central gazebo to Jimmy Amster.

In 1995, Peter Detmold Park became one of the many city parks to include a dog run. Dogs were now able to run unleashed in a fenced-in area at the north end of the park.

STUCK ON FIRST

By the time the East River Drive was renamed the Franklin Delano Roosevelt Drive in 1945, it was well on its way to becoming a continuous limited-access artery stretching the full length of Manhattan's eastern waterfront. The conversion was done in sections. By 1966, cars could enter the six-lane FDR Drive at Battery Park and travel unencumbered by local traffic straight through to 125th Street. Along the way, the Drive was accessed by a series of ramps. A southbound exit ramp was built at East 49th Street and a northbound entrance ramp at East 48th Street.

In April 1987, the city closed the 48th Street ramp, an ostensibly temporary move while the ramp was used to stage heavy equipment for repairs to the FDR Drive. Now, with no northbound entrance to the FDR from 34th Street to 62nd Street, traffic on First Avenue began to back up, often coming to a complete standstill amid blaring horns and exhaust fumes. Residents patiently awaited completion of the repair work.

So it was a shock to neighborhood leaders when two years later, at a public Community Board 6 meeting on a park matter, a planner from the city's Transportation Department mentioned in passing that the city wasn't certain it would ever reopen the ramp.

The casual disclosure set off a firestorm of protest. The entire East Side of Midtown banded together: The Turtle Bay Association, Beekman Place Association, Sutton Area Community, South York Avenue Association, and Community Board 6 were joined by the boards of large apartment buildings along First Avenue, including 100 United Nations Plaza, Plaza 400, and 860–870 United Nations Plaza.

When Lucius Riccio, transportation commissioner under Mayor David Dinkins, met with a standing-room-only crowd to try to explain, the outrage only grew. He listed not one, but four reasons why the ramp would not be reopened: It was structurally unsound; the city didn't have enough money to adequately repair it; it was dangerous because of its left-lane entry; and statistics showed that traffic flows on First Avenue hadn't changed much since the ramp was closed.

Residents were infuriated. "It was obvious to anyone observing First Avenue that the traffic had gotten worse over the past two years," says Bruce Silberblatt, a TBA board member who lived on First Avenue and spearheaded the Turtle Bay community's protest. Neighbors found a strong supporter in City Councilman Robert Dryfoos and together with other elected officials formed the East 48th Street Ramp Task Force. For the next nine years, the task force battled relentlessly to get the ramp back in action.

A professional transportation consultant confirmed to the neighborhood that the bumper-to-bumper traffic was increasing noise and air pollution, and police records showed a dramatic increase in traffic accidents on the avenue since the ramp was shut down. Soon, the ramp closure created another irritant to the neighborhood: Homeless people began to set up a cardboard "shantytown" around the concrete shelter of the now quiet, unused ramp.

Residents kept up the pressure. They rallied at the foot of the 48th Street ramp, marched on City Hall with petitions and placards proclaiming "Stuck on First" and "Pollution Poisons," and at a City Council Transportation Committee hearing in March 1992, laid out their case: Contrary to a city report, there were actually 10,000 more cars each day on the avenue since the ramp closed, and the accident toll had soared. But it was the testimony of a young paramedic for the Emergency Medical Services, Simeon Klebaner, that struck a chord at the hearing. "First Avenue traffic tie-ups were making it tough for me and my co-workers to get our ambulances to accidents on the FDR and the nearby neighborhood," he recalls telling the packed hearing room. "Somebody had to say something."

The City Transportation Department began to soften its stance. By the fall of 1992, the city said it was now willing to approve the repair work if state or federal money could be found to pay for it. In 1993, the ramp reopening seemed likely, using state funds for the estimated $10 to $12 million project. During 1994 and 1995, neighbors waited, cautious but optimistic. But then the area's state senator, Roy Goodman, who had doggedly pursued state funding, delivered bad news: A budget crunch in Albany had eliminated capital spending for the fiscal year.

Next, safety concerns split the community and threatened to delay action even further. Some feared the old ramp design, with its left-hand entry lane, was too dangerous. To build it with a new design could mean added costs and years of delay, something the Turtle Bay community resisted.

The project finally got underway in 1998, more than a decade after the ramp first closed. State funds were freed up and the ramp was to be replaced with a totally new one. It would have a left-hand entry lane, but its longer acceleration distance gave drivers more time to merge with northbound traffic.

After years of delays and false starts, once the project got started, residents were surprised that it was completed eight months ahead of schedule. Traffic started flowing onto the new ramp in October 1998. When Governor George Pataki, then running for his second term, showed up for a well-publicized "photo op" to mark the early reopening, some in the media couldn't help noting that the opening was just 12 days before election day.

"But if that's what it took to get our new ramp up and running, so be it," says Silberblatt. "After more than a decade, we could finally declare victory over gridlock."

The new ramp provided another potential bonus. It was built slightly north of where the old ramp stood, providing space for a pedestrian or bicycle path to a riverfront esplanade, should one be built in the future.

White Christmas

Cabaret singer and songwriter John Wallowitch moved to a 51st Street brownstone near Beekman Place in 1967, unaware that a music legend lived just around the corner. "When someone told me Irving Berlin lived at 17 Beekman, it simply galvanized me. I couldn't believe it!" the Juilliard-trained musician recalled years later.

On Wallowitch's first Christmas Eve in the neighborhood, he was out walking his dog when he passed Irving Berlin's house. He stopped and sang silently, to himself, *White Christmas* and *I'll be Loving You Always*, two of his favorite Berlin tunes. "It was a very emotional experience for me, and it became my own personal Christmas Eve tradition for many years," he said.

Then on Christmas Eve 1983, the year Berlin was 95, Wallowitch asked a group of 17 friends—talented musicians all—to join him for his ritual serenade. "We met at my place and then walked to the corner near Mr. Berlin's house where we sang, out loud this time, *White Christmas*, then *Always*, and then *White Christmas* once again."

The house was dark and they assumed no one was home. Much to their surprise, as they were leaving, the lights throughout the house lit up and a housekeeper came to the door to invite them in. "Mr. Berlin would like to thank you," she said.

"We were simply astonished," said Wallowitch. "Here we were face-to-face with the greatest composer of our lifetime in his own house! He greeted us with his big bright eyes and shook hands with each of the guys and hugged the gals. 'Thank you,' he said. 'That was the nicest Christmas present I ever had.'"

"You can live on an experience like that for a lifetime," said Wallowitch. "It was such an honor."

The group continued to sing outside Berlin's house each Christmas Eve until 1988. The next September, Berlin died at his home at the age of 101. Out of respect, the carolers didn't sing at the house that Christmas Eve. But the tradition resumed in 1990. The serenade became an annual tribute to the memory of Irving Berlin and the more than 40 years he lived at 17 Beekman Place.

CALL ME MADAM

After Irving Berlin's death, the house was put on the market. Neighbors wondered what would happen to it. Some worried that new owners might not appreciate its musical traditions. And so when the buyer was announced—the Government of Luxembourg—the accompanying irony was taken as a good omen. While he lived at No. 17, Berlin had written the words and music to *Call Me Madam*, the musical based on the 1949 appointment of Washington hostess Perle Mesta as the first U.S. ambassador to Luxembourg.

It turned out there was more than irony in Luxembourg's taking over the house. From the start, neighbors could see that Luxembourg House, as it came to be known, would continue to reflect the memory of the beloved composer and his music.

The house would be the combined offices of several government functions, including that of the Consulate General and the Mission to the United Nations. But the offices were located on the upper three levels, leaving the first two floors—the main living areas, including the paneled library where the composer's Steinway piano had stood—much as they were during Berlin's day.

And the musical tradition continued. Over the years, Luxembourg House has become the site of musical events and art shows for the diplomatic corps, neighbors, and friends. "We want to keep alive the memory of Irving Berlin and preserve the rich history of his former home," says Georges Faber, consul general during the early 2000s.

The connection with *Call Me Madam* is more than a simple coincidence, he says. "To this day, Perle Mesta is fondly remembered in Luxembourg. We're proud to have a link to Ms. Mesta through the musical works of the magnificent Irving Berlin."

As for Wallowitch's caroling friends, each Christmas Eve the Luxembourg House has awaited their arrival, enjoyed their music, and then invited them in for holiday drinks. Wallowitch, who died in 2007 at the age of 81, was pleased with his new neighbors at 17 Beekman. "Luxembourg House is truly honoring the Berlin legacy," he said.

Host to the World

While Luxembourg may have secured one of Turtle Bay's most storied houses for its offices, it is only one of more than 125 U.N. missions and scores of consulates that line the streets and avenues of Turtle Bay. Thousands of U.N. diplomats and staff live in the area and on any given day, hundreds of visiting international government and business people meet in offices within walking distance of U.N. headquarters. The neighborhood has become a true crossroads of the world.

The United Nations is ever-present in Turtle Bay, from the ritual of raising the 192 flags of the U.N.'s member countries along First Avenue each weekday morning, to the pomp and circumstance of the annual U.N. General Assembly session each fall.

As the decade of the 1980s came to a close, U.N. and city officials were already starting to plan for the United Nations' 50th anniversary session in 1995. The celebration would bring together the largest gathering of heads of state in history. On a single day, the leaders of more than 180 nations would be in Turtle Bay. (Although technically, once on the U.N. campus, they would be in international territory.)

While preparations for handling so many national leaders at one time was an enormous feat, the logistics and security arrangements were not unlike what goes on every year, when typically at least 80 heads of state gather in Turtle Bay for the opening session of the Assembly.

A Coast Guard flotilla keeps vigil from the East River; police helicopters fly overhead; streets are closed to vehicular traffic, some even to pedestrians; and security checkpoints are set up throughout Turtle Bay. The avenue in front of the United Nations is lined with television news trucks, a permanent fixture for the duration of the session.

As a steady stream of motorcades moves up First Avenue, presidents and prime ministers are dropped off at the U.N.'s front door, to be picked up later and delivered to nearby hotels, all of which are booked at least a year in advance of the big U.N. meeting. The Waldorf-Astoria—where the Waldorf Towers is the residence of the U.S. president whenever he is in New York—and the U.N. Plaza Hotel, directly across the street from the United Nations, each is likely to have some 30 heads of state in residence at the same time. For the two-week opening session of the U.N. General Assembly, Turtle Bay finds itself, literally, at the center of the world's stage.

Many in the neighborhood find it exhilarating. Others say that stalled traffic, continual "gridlock alerts," shrieking sirens, unruly protests, and even over-booked restaurants only add to another long-time community concern—that diplomatic immunity allows foreign diplomats to ignore parking tickets, rent agreements, and ordinary bills.

But on one point no one disagrees: Since 1946, when John D. Rockefeller Jr. bought an 18-acre industrial site on the East River waterfront and donated it to the United Nations for its headquarters, the world body has in many ways defined Turtle Bay. This would be evident yet again in the 1990s when neighbors proudly welcomed a new "central park" to their midst, a parcel of parkland that was a direct by-product of the United Nations' early development in Midtown Manhattan.

5. New and Renewed: The 1990s

Rich people don't like losing their view—that is pure and simple what this is all about.
—Donald Trump, in a retort to East Midtown neighbors who argued that his 861-foot residential tower, more than 350 feet taller than the nearby U.N. Secretariat, was out of scale with surrounding buildings.

A Plaza Created

For Rita Carpanini, who was born on East 49th Street in the 1930s and lived there most of her life, there was only one problem with the United Nations moving into her neighborhood. "I didn't like what happened to my church," she says.

Rita's church was St. Boniface Roman Catholic Church, a small red brick structure built in 1858 at the southeast corner of 47th Street and Second Avenue. The rectory and parochial school were just east of the church. In 1947, as the United Nations' architectural team firmed up its plans, the City Planning Commission looked at ways to develop the surrounding area. It fell to Robert Moses, then city construction coordinator, to come up with a proposal. Moses focused mainly on ways in which traffic would flow around the area. His plans included widening the eastern end of 42nd Street and constructing a tunnel under First Avenue between 41st and 48th Streets to ease traffic on the top level. In addition, he wanted to create a grand entrance to the United Nations by broadening 47th

Street between First and Second Avenues. To do so, the buildings on the entire south side of 47th Street would have to be razed. That included St. Boniface.

St. Boniface worshippers fought the demolition. But the city's Board of Estimate approved the plan and in 1950, the church came down, along with its rectory, the school and some factory buildings to the east. Ironically, and sadly, by the time the demolition finally took place, the United Nations architectural plans called for the U.N. entrance to be further south on First Avenue, not even accessible from the "grand boulevard" envisioned by Moses.

The demolition created an odd block. A narrow strip of empty land now ran along the unsightly backsides of 46th Street tenements and a 17-story office building. North of the strip, a tree-lined median separated two traffic lanes, remnants of what was meant to be the boulevard to the U.N.'s front door.

In 1961, the strip of land was named Dag Hammarskjold Plaza in honor of the U.N. Secretary General who died in a plane crash in the Congo that year. In the next few years, the city considered a series of sculptural amenities for the narrow Plaza, including a tall pylon of marble, gold leaf, and stainless steel, and another that called for a bronze and white granite memorial to Hammarskjold, centered in the Plaza against a backdrop of trees and shrubs. Then in 1964, the most stunning of all the designs was proposed—an arched pedestrian bridge that would rise over First Avenue from the east end of the Plaza, turn south above the avenue, and end in the United Nations Gardens on the other side. It too was to be a memorial to Dag Hammarskjold. None of the designs ever materialized, stymied by a lack of funding and practicality.

Again in 1968 the Plaza attracted attention when, as part of the embattled U.N. expansion plan, an elevated walkway was to lead from the center of the Plaza to a U.N. "super block." But the expansion plan was never approved, and the walkway never built.

Then in 1970, a Plaza upgrade was announced that seemingly could resolve its future for the next 125 years. At the time, developer Harry Macklowe was marketing a new 15-story office building at 866 Second Avenue (later named Two Dag Hammarskjold Plaza). The building's north arcade abutted the Plaza. Macklowe reached an agreement with the city to build a sculpture garden on the Plaza that would adjoin his building's arcade. Under the plan, Macklowe paid for construction of the 10,000-square-foot sculpture garden, agreed to maintain it for 125 years and supply it with changing exhibits of contemporary sculpture. In press releases and interviews, the deal was touted as a "win-win:" Macklowe got a more attractive approach to his building, and the City Parks Department resolved at least part of the quandary over what to do with Dag Hammarskjold Plaza.

The community never liked the sculpture garden. Residents felt its brick and concrete platforms discouraged the general public from using the area, and many thought the modern sculpture more "unusual" than "artful."

Macklowe later sold the building and over the years, the sculpture garden fell into disrepair, its barren platforms serving as little more than shelter for the homeless.

The Plaza became a neighborhood eyesore. Turtle Bay residents generally avoided it. Its main attraction was as a staging area for protests and rallies. "Sad looking," some said. "A menace and a blight to the neighborhood," said others.

PLANNING FOR PLAZA RENEWAL

By the early 1980s, the Parks Department again was focusing on the Plaza. Preliminary architectural plans were drawn up and discussed, and neighbors began to seriously recognize the potential that the narrow strip of land represented to the community. They also knew that transforming the by-now derelict acreage into a welcoming park would be a significant challenge.

Bronson Binger, assistant parks commissioner at the time, was in charge of capital projects. Like his boss Henry Stern, who was named parks commissioner in 1983, Binger was eager to see the Plaza plans move forward. Binger knew the neighborhood well. He was the grandson of Charlotte Martin, creator of the Turtle Bay Gardens complex in the early 1920s. Now, 60 years later, Binger would himself play a role in rejuvenating Turtle Bay.

Binger was impressed with a young college student, George Vellonakis, who worked in the Parks Department during the summers. It wasn't long before Vellonakis, who earned a landscape architecture degree from New York City College in 1984, joined Binger's staff as a full-time employee. Soon, Vellonakis found himself with his first Parks challenge: He was asked to design a new plan for Dag Hammarskjold Plaza.

"The Plaza is an unusual park space," says Vellonakis. "Being directly across from the United Nations, it's an official forum area for protests and demonstrations, and so Community Board 6 felt strongly that we needed to stick with a plan that used a great deal of hard surface, yet provided a warm and inviting atmosphere."

In June 1989, the Vellonakis plan was formally introduced to the neighborhood at a Community Board 6 public meeting. The proposal—which called for removing the sculpture garden platforms and then landscaping the entire Plaza with a garden, trees, and fountains—was greeted warmly. But another element of the plan, and an important one, sparked controversy.

In order to broaden the narrow Plaza into a more usable space, the city's Transportation Department had agreed that one of the two roadways that Robert Moses planned as part of a grand boulevard to the United Nations 40 years earlier was no longer needed. By eliminating the southern roadway, the Plaza could be increased by one third, to 1.6 acres.

It may have sounded like a logical suggestion to some. But it set off a firestorm of debate. The street was a crosstown bus route—the M27 and M50 bus lines—and the eastern end of 47th Street served as a layover point, an area where buses queued up to await their next trip.

The plan called for the one remaining roadway to consist of two lanes of westbound automobile traffic and one lane of eastbound bus traffic. But 47th Street residents and businesses said it would be dangerous to have westbound and eastbound traffic on the same roadway. And some didn't like the idea of rejuvenating the Plaza under any circumstances. They felt it would only attract bigger and louder demonstrations, and provide a more comfortable resting place for the homeless.

With no funding available for the $2.9 million project, the controversy faded into the background for the next few years. But behind the scenes, Turtle Bay leaders continued to push to get money for a Plaza renovation.

Finally in 1994, more than half of the projected budget was appropriated, a three-way funding split among the offices of City Councilman Andrew Eristoff, Manhattan Borough President Ruth Messinger, and Mayor Rudolph Giuliani. The project would be done in three phases. In the first phase, the owners of Two Dag Hammarskjold Plaza agreed to remove the old sculpture garden platforms and renovate the area in return for the city releasing them from the long-term maintenance agreement they had inherited from the previous owner. The second phase called for the rest of the space to be renovated and landscaped. The third phase—the "hot potato" question of how to handle the roadways along 47th Street—was put on hold.

On a sunny October 12, 1994, community leaders and elected officials picked up their shovels for the ceremonial groundbreaking of Phase One and Two. On hand were Parks Commissioner Henry Stern, joined by U.S. Congresswoman Carolyn Maloney, State Assemblyman John Ravitz, Councilman Andrew Eristoff, TBA President Bill Curtis, Community Board 6 Chairman Lou Sepersky, and Anne Saxon-Hersh, president of a new group formed to support the Plaza with private funds, the Friends of Dag Hammarskjold Plaza.

But the controversy over the buses continued. The Turtle Bay Association wanted them rerouted. "How can we expect to have a park-like atmosphere with buses rumbling down the street and idling their polluted fumes during layovers at First Avenue and the Plaza?" asked Curtis. But the TBA also wanted to be sure that bus service in the community would not be diminished. Curtis and Gary Papush, chairman of the Parks Committee of Community Board 6, suggested that they be rerouted to 42nd Street. Not only would that eliminate the buses on 47th Street, but Curtis knew from talking with Tudor City residents that they would welcome the convenience of bus service so nearby. But the Metropolitan Transportation Authority said the longer routing would be too costly in terms of time and fuel.

When it was suggested that the buses use either 46th, 48th, or 50th Streets, the ultimate "battle of the blocks" broke out. Reporting on a March 1997 Community Board 6 public hearing on the matter, the *New York Observer* put it this way: "No eyes were gouged, but long-time Midtown neighbors tore into each other with bare-knuckled rhetoric and oratorical shin kicks."

Meanwhile, work continued on the Plaza. The garden, which runs along its south side, was shaping up to be a glorious part of the project. Planted with flowering dogwood, birch and redwood trees, and mountain laurel, it provided a dense green backdrop that softened the Plaza's asphalt pavers.

George Vellonakis recalls being in the garden one morning to update Millie Margiotta, a TBA Board member, on the project. "She turned to me and said, 'I wish our neighbor Katharine Hepburn could see this. She would be so pleased.' "

Margiotta, who had worked hard to get the Plaza project moving forward, was a lifelong admirer of Hepburn and knew the famous actress was an avid gardener. Hepburn, now in her late 80s, had recently moved from her town house on 49th Street to her family's home in Fenwick, Connecticut.

"Before long, we were talking about naming the garden in honor of Ms. Hepburn," Vellonakis remembers. Margiotta communicated with Hepburn's advisor, Erik Hanson, to learn that Hepburn liked the idea, and Margiotta got a speedy approval from Parks Commissioner Stern.

The new "Katharine Hepburn Garden" was completed in time for the actress's 90th birthday on May 12, 1997. Although she was not able to attend, scores of her friends and colleagues, and hundreds of neighbors, gathered that morning to formally dedicate the tranquil oasis of flowers and plants. Stage and screen luminaries Julie Harris, Garson Kanin, Marian Seldes, and Sam Waterston were at the garden, as was Anthony Harvey, who directed Hepburn in her Academy Award–winning performance in *The Lion in Winter* and who himself was nominated for an Oscar for the same movie. "Such a lovely garden, and it's so appropriate that it be named for a true romantic like Kate," he said in remarks to the guests.

Meanwhile, renovation plans for the remainder of the Plaza were dependent on the bus route. The stalemate continued.

In November 1997, Mayor Giuliani, whose office had committed to paying for one third of the project's final phase, abruptly withdrew support. No one was quite sure why. Curtis called an emergency meeting of community leaders and elected officials. The TBA remained convinced that the buses should go to 42nd Street, but now that they were faced with no action on the plan at all, the TBA and Community Board 6 looked seriously at compromise alternatives. "No question about it, the community wants this park, and we want to see the job done right," Curtis said at the time.

As Curtis and the community strategized on what to do, a new player had "moved" to the neighborhood. Developer Donald Trump had recently purchased the Engineering Center on 47th Street across the street from the Plaza and was reported to be considering a luxury residential building on the site. During a meeting with Curtis and other community leaders to discuss his building plans, Trump made it clear that he wanted to see the Plaza renovation completed. "I'll call Rudy," he told the group.

Then Katharine Hepburn weighed in. Through Erik Hanson, she threatened to pull her name from her newly dedicated garden unless the entire Plaza project was completed. "If there is not an acceptable compromise, we do not want her name associated with the project," Hanson told the press a week after Giuliani's announcement. "When the garden was named in her honor, we were told that the street would be narrowed and the park enlarged. That is what we agreed to."

In April 1998, Mayor Giuliani paid an afternoon visit to the Plaza site. Parks Commissioner Stern accompanied him. "He'd heard from so many people—pro and con—that he felt he needed to 'go to the scene,' to see for himself the dimensions of the park, and what the bus situation was all about," Stern remembers.

Next, Giuliani agreed to meet with the community at a town hall meeting. "There, we made it abundantly clear that we wanted the plaza completed soon, and in a way that maximized the space available," said Bill Curtis, whose TBA organization hosted the meeting.

On Wednesday, September 23, Giuliani and Stern returned to Dag Hammarskjold Plaza. This time, Giuliani held a press conference to announce that the project would go forward. Construction was to begin the following Monday. And the buses? They would never again run along 47th Street. Instead, the mayor and the MTA agreed they would be routed to 42nd Street, the spot suggested many years earlier by Bill Curtis and Gary Papush.

When the new Dag Hammarskjold Plaza officially opened on August 18, 1999, it almost immediately became the treasured centerpiece of Turtle Bay. With a large domed pavilion at its west end, smaller lattice pavilions with six reflecting pools of cascading water along the south wall, garden greenery, park benches, and a café concession, the Plaza beckons neighbors from throughout Midtown. Summertime events—dance performances, concerts, and art shows—are sponsored by the Friends of Dag Hammarskjold Plaza and the Turtle Bay Association. And each Wednesday all year long, the city's Greenmarket is open at the Plaza's west end, with stalls selling farm-fresh produce, meats, baked goods, and flowers.

A PARK BENCH

In September 1997, soon after the Katharine Hepburn Garden opened, architect George Vellonakis and Millie Margiotta were invited to have lunch with Hepburn at her home in Connecticut. The 19-room white brick house overlooking Long Island Sound stood on the site that had been the Hepburn family's vacation retreat since Katharine Hepburn was just five years old. Throughout her life, she spent many long weekends there. Now she was living at Fenwick permanently.

Hepburn greeted Margiotta and Vellonakis in her comfortable living room in front of the fireplace, in which—as she did every day of the year, no matter what the weather—she had a fire burning. Sitting in a well-worn overstuffed chair, she wore khakis and a white turtleneck sweater, her hair done up in a bun. At the bay windows overlooking the Sound were pots of flowers, lined up in four neat rows. They were colorful, well-cared-for flowers.

As was the custom when Hepburn entertained guests at Fenwick, lunch was served in the living room on snack trays. Soup came first, then a chicken salad, cranberry juice, and vanilla ice cream. Margiotta and Vellonakis sat on either side of Hepburn. "We talked about gardening and the park. George explained to her the design of the garden, and the kinds of plants he thought would do well there," Margiotta says, "And she had some ideas of her own. Oh, how she loved her gardening."

Vellonakis presented Hepburn with a replica of the green-and-white Parks Department sign—Katharine Hepburn Garden—that hangs at the entrance to the Garden at Dag Hammarskjold Plaza. She smiled. "Place it over by my flowers at the window, dear," she said to Vellonakis. He carefully leaned it up against one of the terra cotta pots.

Later, as they left the house accompanied by Erik Hanson, Vellonakis and Margiotta spotted an old park bench under some pine trees on the front lawn. "That is one of Miss Hepburn's favorite reading spots here at Fenwick," Hanson told them.

Vellonakis looked shocked, as only a Parks Department employee might be. "That is a New York City Parks Department bench!" he exclaimed. "How did she get that?"

Indeed, the bench was the elongated wood and hooped metal style seen in public parks throughout the city. Originally designed for the 1939 World's Fair, today it's simply referred to as the '39 World's Fair bench. "Well, I think her brother—a real collector, he was—'found' it years ago and brought it here. Miss Hepburn has always really liked it," Hanson replied.

Vellonakis and Margiotta couldn't forget the bench. They began to envision it amidst the trees and plantings in the new Katharine Hepburn Garden at Dag Hammarskjold Plaza.

Katharine Hepburn died at her home in Fenwick in June 2003, at the age of 96. A year later, Sotheby's held an auction of her personal property. As the auction house prepared the items for sale, Margiotta called Hanson.

"The park bench is at Sotheby's scheduled to be auctioned," he told her. "But let me know if you want me to take it out of the exhibit."

Margiotta didn't have to think twice about the offer. "I believe I was on the phone with the Parks Department to arrange to pick it up even before I could say 'yes' to Erik!" she says.

In June 2004, Hepburn's park bench was formally unveiled at its new spot in the Katharine Hepburn Garden. An inscription above it reads: "In loving memory of Katharine Houghton Hepburn, 1907–2003."

New and Renewed

Tumultuous Times for a Landmark

In the years after Amster Yard and Turtle Bay Gardens were designated New York City Landmarks, seven other Turtle Bay sites joined the list. The former home of Modernist architect William Lescaze, converted from a brownstone into a modern town house at 211 East 48th Street in 1934, was named a landmark in 1976. Two other larger Turtle Bay properties were given landmark status in the late 1980s: the former Beaux-Arts Institute of Design and the dual Beaux-Arts Apartments on East 44th Street, built in 1928 and 1930, respectively.

The former Panhellenic Tower at 3 Mitchell Place, by architect John Mead Howells, was added to the list in 1998. It had been constructed in 1928 as a women's hotel and later converted to a conventional hotel, the Beekman Tower. And in 2000, the former Rockefeller/Museum of Modern Art Guest House—an East 52nd Street carriage house renovated by Philip Johnson in 1950—was named a landmark, as was 314 East 53rd Street, a clapboard house which, like the neighboring house at 312 that was landmarked earlier, had been built in 1866 shortly before frame houses in the area were outlawed as fire threats.

But of all the culturally significant sites in Turtle Bay, perhaps none encountered more tumult over the years than did Amster Yard.

In 1970, just four years after Jimmy Amster won landmark status for Amster Yard, he was back in the news with a pioneering move being watched in preservation circles throughout the country. Amster was asking city permission to sell the air rights over his low-rise houses— the unused development rights—to a developer who planned to build a high-rise office tower on Third Avenue adjacent to his property. The air rights transfer would allow the builder, Laird Properties, to add some 30,000 square feet of space to what was otherwise permitted on the site. Recent amendments to the city's zoning resolution made such a sale possible, but no owner of a landmarked property had ever before proposed it. Approvals were needed from the Landmarks Preservation Commission, City Planning Commission, and the Board of Estimate.

Preservationists strongly supported the sale. It would set a precedent that could assure the long-term survival of historically and culturally valuable sites that might otherwise be threatened if owners were to receive tempting offers to sell.

As part of the deal, the developer agreed to make design concessions so the tower's ground level would be in harmony with Amster Yard. The exterior facing the Yard would be dark red brick rather than glass and steel, and "mansarded" bay windows would complement the Yard's shingled mansard roof.

The transfer plan also had the firm backing of Community Board 6 and the Turtle Bay Association, and it quickly moved through the city approval process.

But the air rights transfer between Amster and Laird Properties never took place. Economic pressures had brought office construction along Third Avenue almost to a halt. The developer abandoned plans for the building.

A May 25, 1971, letter from Landmarks Preservation Commission Chairman Harmon Goldstone to Amster shortly after the deal fell through reflects preservationists' thinking at the time. Goldstone called the transfer "a significant pioneering venture," and wrote, "We regret that changing economic conditions led the developer . . . to abandon his plans, but we are confident that this imaginative proposal will appeal to another builder."

The economic downturn lasted well into the 1970s. It would be almost 10 years before another builder, this time Cohen Brothers Realty & Construction, would use the Amster Yard air rights.

The Cohen Brothers also acquired air rights from Smith and Wollensky, a two-story restaurant at the northeast corner of 49th Street and Third Avenue, the site where an earlier steakhouse, Manny Wolf's, had operated since the 1930s. The Cohens planned a 35-story building with more than 550,000 square feet of office space and 27,000 square feet of retail space in an enclosed pedestrian mall. Four floors of the building—its address was 805 Third Avenue but it was to be known as the Crystal Pavilion—were dependent on the developer qualifying for a discretionary floor-area "bonus" for including a public amenity in the plan, the covered pedestrian area. The Cohen Brothers expected the bonus to be approved and, in one of the tightest office markets in the city's history, the firm easily rented commercial space for its planned 35-story building.

But the community objected to the building's height. The Turtle Bay Association and Community Board 6 said its shadows would rob sunlight from the small Greenacre Park on 51st Street, and they felt strongly that the public space, tucked away and not readily accessible to the public, did not merit the additional four floors. Preservationist groups agreed, saying they saw no public benefit from the sale of Amster Yard's air rights.

In May 1980, the City Planning Commission sided with the community's objections and took away two of the bonus floors. A few weeks later, the Board of Estimate went even further, denying any bonus at all for the atrium area. The decisions sent Crystal Pavilion architects Emery Roth & Sons scurrying back to their drawing boards and the developer into tough—and widely reported—renegotiations with tenants who had already rented space that now would not be built. The Crystal Pavilion opened in 1982 with 31 floors, four less than originally planned.

Meanwhile, its air rights now utilized, Amster Yard would continue to stay on the list of preservationists' concerns. Almost 20 years later, the Yard was in the headlines again, this time with its very existence at issue.

Robert Moyer, Jimmy Amster's partner for 41 years, stayed on at Amster Yard after Amster died in 1986. Other residents gradually moved and finally in 1992, Moyer, by then the Yard's last remaining resident, moved also. Amster Yard continued to be the address of a couple of small businesses for the next few years. But by 1998 the Yard, which Amster had sold several years before his death, had fallen into foreclosure. The neighborhood watched anxiously to see what would happen to the garden haven that for years had been an anchor of the area. An affiliate of Credit Suisse First Boston that specialized in distressed properties soon bought Amster Yard, then re-sold it within 15 months. The identity of the new buyer delighted neighbors and preservationists alike: Instituto Cervantes, the highly regarded cultural arm of the Spanish government, had acquired the property to serve as a center of art, music, and education.

"This was what we had hoped for," said Bill Curtis, whose TBA organization had watched sadly as the Yard declined in recent years. "Amster Yard would now be preserved and open to the public for cultural events."

Curtis and his neighbors were aware that the Institute had received approval from the city's Landmarks Preservation Commission to make alterations to the property. But they weren't prepared for the extent of the changes, or the way they would unfold.

Instituto Cervantes had been given the go-ahead to excavate for a basement auditorium and to demolish two of the four structures surrounding the courtyard. The buildings and courtyard would then be restored to their original 1940s appearance.

What actually happened was quite different. After work started, some walls of the small courtyard houses apparently were deemed to be too unsafe to renovate, and virtually all the courtyard structures were torn down. Alex Herrera of the New York Landmarks Conservancy, a leading preservation advocacy group that holds a preservation easement on the property, discovered the demolition on a routine visit to the site in the spring of 2002.* He was stunned.

"We still don't know how this could have happened without the Institute getting approval from the Landmarks Preservation Commission, and without the Conservancy being alerted," Herrera says today. "It is true that the condition of the old walls was bad, but as part owner of the site, we clearly should have been alerted. We were not."

Neighbors, too, were upset over the loss. And they were particularly unhappy when the dirty, noisy construction work dragged on for nearly two years. The Institute said it was committed to rebuilding the demolished buildings, but preservationists soon were referring to the "end of Amster Yard."

Moyer, who had moved several blocks south of Turtle Bay, heard only news reports of what was happening to his home of nearly five decades. "I simply couldn't bear to walk by," he says.

Then in September 2003, shortly before Spain's Crown Prince Felipe was to fly to New York to inaugurate the new "Instituto Cervantes at Amster Yard," the Institute's director, Antonio Martinez, invited Moyer and Elinor Jay, who had been Amster's assistant for many years, to return to Amster Yard. Moyer says he accepted reluctantly. "I feared what I would find in the place where I had lived so happily for so many years," he says.

---

* A preservation easement, a legal agreement between a property owner and qualified preservation group, is intended to protect a site by restricting future changes or development on the property.

To the contrary, he was pleasantly surprised. "As soon as I walked through the front gate, I felt like I had returned home," he says.

Indeed, the Amster Yard to which Moyer and Jay returned was a near-precise replica of the original. Although clearly not a restoration—only the façades of the street-front buildings and some decorative ironwork were preserved—even some of the harshest critics were surprised with the results. Every exterior detail was expertly reproduced: the mansard shingled roof, eclectic corrugated detailing, roof trellis and, of course, the Elsie de Wolfe–inspired "trick" mirror at the end of the garden.

The controversy among preservationists never completely died down. But Moyer doesn't agree with the critics. "It's a magnificent replica, and by modernizing and enlarging the original space, Jimmy's courtyard home is now available for so many more people to enjoy."*

FIRST AVENUE: OLD AND NEW

After One United Nations Plaza—the UNDC office and hotel tower—opened in 1975, Midtown's First Avenue saw relatively little new construction for several years. At 48th Street, 100 United Nations Plaza, a 52-story condominium with a distinctive triangular rooftop, was completed in 1986. But most of the neighborhood's attention was focused on one of the avenue's oldest buildings, a former public school house built in 1892. Designed by the Board of Education's staff architect George Debevoise, the Romanesque Revival building, at 931 First Avenue and 51st Street, stood almost precisely on the site of what had once been James Beekman's 18th-century house, "Mount Pleasant."

The four-story building was designated P.S. 135 (originally P.S. 35) and in more recent years had been used as space for the United Nations

---

* Amster Yard, at 211–215 East 49th Street, is open to the public every day except Sunday.

International School and then later as a private school. It was in the late 1970s that area residents learned that the city planned to tear down the attractive yellow brick building with its brownstone trim and ornamental roof detailing. The site was to be sold to a developer. A determined group of preservation-minded neighbors, from groups including Community Board 6, Turtle Bay Association, Beekman Place Association, and Sutton Area Community, formed the Coalition to Save 931.

Community Board 6 asked the newest member of its Land Use Committee, Brenda Levin, to head the effort. Brenda took her role seriously. "I think people were amazed that we were able to save this beloved distinguished building from the wrecking ball," she says.

Working closely with Levin were Richard Eyen, who lived in the Sutton area and who also later headed the Coalition; Bill Curtis; and Buddy Radisch from Beekman Place.

The group's success was not immediate. But when it won a spot for the school house on the National Register of Historic Places, it seemed more likely they would be triumphant. Shortly thereafter, the city's Board of Estimate voted unanimously to support the Coalition's proposition that the building was worth preserving.

In the fall of 1983, the city announced it planned to put the school house and its land on the auction block, with the condition that the exterior of the 90-year-old building be preserved. Thus began a series of aborted attempts to convert the building into a space that could satisfy neighbors, the city, preservationists, and developers alike. In the interim, the city converted the school into a temporary shelter for homeless women.

Over the next 10 years, the property was auctioned a total of three times, only to have each of the deals eventually fall through. When the building and its site were finally offered as a negotiated sale in 1996, a resolution seemed close at hand. Within a few years, developer Dennis

A. Herman moved ahead with plans to build an apartment high rise within the exterior walls of the original 1892 school. "It was a difficult job," says Herman, "First, the asbestos removal took a long time, and then the old walls—some 15–24 inches thick—had to be stabilized with steel girders."

In 2004, more than two decades after the Coalition to Save 931 began its crusade, the 20-story Beekman Regent, designed by New York's noted residential architect Costas Kondylis, opened with 64 apartments. The structure is an entirely new building within the walls of the old school, with four distinct apartment designs. Ten of the apartments are loft-like dwellings directly behind the original exterior. A bronze plaque on the southeast corner of the building reads: "On this site, from 1763 to 1874, stood Mount Pleasant . . . used by Lord Howe during the Revolutionary War . . ."

About the same time the Beekman Regent was completed, another Kondylis-designed building opened across the avenue, the Grand Beekman at 400 East 51st Street. New from the ground up, the 32-story building has 89 condominium apartments.

But it was a third Costas Kondylis building—just three blocks south from the Beekman "duo"—that caused the loudest outcry of any construction project in the neighborhood's history. In the fall of 1998, developer Donald Trump announced that he would build the tallest residential building in the world on the site of the 1960s Engineering Center at First Avenue between 47th and 48th Streets. He asked Kondylis to design a slender tower that would rise 861 feet, the equivalent of some 90 stories (although the apartments' high ceilings reduced the actual floors to 72). Trump had quietly bought up unused air rights from nearby institutions along 47th Street, including the Japan Society and the Church of the Holy Family, and air rights from two garages on 48th Street. Their consolidation, along with a small public plaza area incorporated in his plans, had allowed him to obtain city permits to begin construction without a public review.

Neighbors were stunned. They had known Trump planned to build on the site, but the extravagant height seemed like an "ego trip" to many. The community believed the building was simply too tall and intrusive for the area, and that it would break an unwritten rule that no building should dwarf the nearby 39-story, 505-foot-high United Nations Secretariat. "If anything deserves to be that prominent, it's the U.N., not Donald Trump," Community Board 6 Land Use Chair Ed Rubin was quoted as saying at the time.

Area neighbors banded together. A well-financed Coalition for Responsible Development, led by some of the wealthier residents of 860–870 United Nations Plaza, along with the TBA and virtually every Midtown neighborhood group, began a public relations and legal campaign to force a reduction in the building's height.

The visibility of the issue was raised when TBA Board member and former CBS executive Blair Clark enlisted the support of retired CBS anchorman Walter Cronkite, who had recently moved to Turtle Bay. Donald Elliott, prominent attorney and former City Planning Commission chairman in the Lindsay administration, was hired to fight the project on legal grounds.

Elliott argued that the block from which the air rights were obtained was divided into two zoning districts, and the transfer of rights from one to another was not permitted under the city's zoning regulations. Further, he argued that the building height should have been dictated by the zoning restriction of the area from which three-quarters of the air rights had been obtained. That would have meant "tower-on-base" construction, resulting in a shorter building.

While the legal arguments were complex, the "war of words" in the media was succinct. The fact that the tall tower would obstruct at least part of the views of some of those protesting gave the never-reticent Donald Trump a quotable media message: "Rich people don't like losing their view—that is pure and simple what this is all about," Trump said over and over again.

Appeals to the city's Board of Standards and Appeals, State Supreme Court, and Appellate Division proved fruitless. By the time the case was heard by the Appellate Division, construction was well underway, already above the 50-story level.

The 861-foot Trump World Tower, with its bronze glass façade, opened its doors in 2001 as the world's tallest residential building. (Within months, Trump's building lost its title to a slightly taller Tower Palace Three in Seoul, Korea; then to an 883-foot residence in Dubai; and soon to several others.)

The Trump Tower and the two other Costas Kondylis–designed buildings were not the only buildings transforming First Avenue in the late 1990s and early 2000s. In 1998, the 23-story German U.N. mission went up between 48th and 49th Streets. Within a few years, the 12-story Anti-Defamation League building at the corner of 46th Street (first opened as the Carnegie Endowment building) was bought and razed for a new high rise. And in 2005, the U.S. Mission to the United Nations, at the corner of 45th Street, was torn down to be replaced with a more secure 27-story tower, its protective façade a glaring reminder of U.S. concerns in a post–September 11 New York.

6. PLANNING FOR TOMORROW: THE EARLY 2000s

I can think of no more stirring symbol of man's humanity to man than a fire truck.
—Author Kurt Vonnegut, in a 2001 tribute to Turtle Bay firefighters.

REMEMBERING

As they did each workday, the firefighters of Engine Company 8, Ladder Company 2, Battalion 8 arrived early at their East 51st Street firehouse for the start of the 9:00 a.m. shift. Over morning coffee, they talked about the day's news, the Mets' chances against the Pirates that night, the weather forecast—clear and sunny, a near-perfect September day. They could hear the morning television news shows in the background. At 8:49 a.m., a CNN bulletin broke in: The North Tower of the World Trade Center had been hit by an airplane.

Minutes later, an alarm came into the firehouse. Ladder Company 2 was to respond immediately to the World Trade Center site. Captain Fred Ill and five men from Ladder 2—joined by Battalion 8 Chief Tom DeAngelis, his aide, and two firefighters about to go home after working their overnight shift—sped out of the firehouse. Just as their truck turned onto 51st Street, news came that the second tower had been struck.

As they drove south along the West Side Highway, the 10 men began to receive radio reports giving them the first indication of the disaster and devastation that awaited them.

Soon, another alarm came in to the East 51st Street firehouse.

Engine Company 8 was to respond to a report of suspicious smoke at Lexington Avenue and 14th Street. When they got to 14th Street, they quickly determined that no fire threatened, and Engine 8 assumed they would be sent downtown to the World Trade Center site. But by now, with so many firefighters diverted to the Towers, coverage was needed back in the Midtown area. The Manhattan dispatcher ordered Engine Company 8 to return to Turtle Bay.

At the firehouse, they awaited news from Ladder 2 and Battalion 8. Families and friends started phoning. "They called over and over again," says Captain Bill Dudley, a 30-year fire department veteran and commanding officer of Engine 8. Like so many firefighters around the city, Captain Dudley had come in on his day off when he first heard the news. He took most of the calls. "I tried to sound reassuring, but as the day wore on, that got pretty tough."

By 4:00 p.m., with still no word from their colleagues, Captain Dudley drove downtown with four other firefighters and Robert Cantillo, a retired Battalion 8 commander who had come back to help. For three hours they searched amid the dust, debris, and chaos. They found no sign of their comrades. "We began to face the fact that surely we would have gotten some phone message, something, to let us know if they were O.K.," Captain Dudley recalls.

The six drove back to the Turtle Bay firehouse. In the early evening, a fellow fireman called to say he had spotted Ladder Company 2's fire truck parked on West Street. It was empty of all its gear and a windshield was broken. But it was drivable. It was decided to bring the truck back home to 51st Street.

"When I saw that truck turn into the firehouse—a ghost-like appearance, empty and covered in heavy white dust and debris—I think that is when I knew . . ." Captain Dudley's voice fades.

On an October evening a few weeks later, several hundred Turtle Bay residents gathered at Dag Hammarskjold Plaza to remember the nearly 3,000 victims of September 11, and to honor the 10 brave firefighters from the 51st Street firehouse.

Author Kurt Vonnegut, Turtle Bay resident, spoke. In early 2000, he had survived a smoky fire in his Turtle Bay brownstone. Now, his simple but poignant words of remembrance brought a hush to the gathering:

> In the entire history of the Fire Department of the City of New York, I have been told, about seven-hundred firefighters have lost their lives in the line of duty. Greater love hath no man than this, that a man lay down his life for his friends. So says the Bible. After the calamity of September eleventh, the *New York Post* asked me for a comment. And I said, "I can think of no more stirring symbol of man's humanity to man than a fire truck."
>
> I myself had my life and our house saved by our local firefighters two years ago. Engine Company 8, Ladder Company 2, Battalion 8. Whether some who did that for me and my wife, Jill, and our daughter, Lily, are dead now, I have not dared to ask.
>
> The body of my speech, such as it is, is sort of a prayer. Some of you may want to bow your heads. That's optional. OK, so here we go:
>
> Chief Tom DeAngelis, dead at fifty.
>
> Captain Fred Ill, dead at forty-seven.
>
> Firefighter Mike Clarke, dead at twenty-seven, the kid of the bunch.
>
> Firefighter George DiPasquale, dead at thirty-four.
>
> Firefighter Dan Harlin, dead at fifty-two.
>
> Firefighter Tom McCann, dead at forty-one

Firefighter Carl Molinaro, dead at thirty-two.

Firefighter Dennis Mulligan, dead at thirty-two.

Firefighter Rob Parro, dead at thirty-five.

Firefighter Denis Germain, dead at thirty-two.

All but two left widows and children. Firefighter Carl Molinaro left a widow and a son, Carl, only two months old, and a daughter age two. Sabrina Molinaro.

Now the first names alone: Tom . . . Fred . . . Mike . . . Dennis . . . Rob . . . George . . . Dan . . . another Tom . . . Carl . . . and another Denis.

Thank you, sirs. God bless you. Amen.

Thus ends my prayer. I have only one further thought, which is this one: It is daylight in Afghanistan. There are many unwelcome fires there, and many, many human beings are trying to put them out.

I thank you for your attention.[2]

After September 11, Vonnegut often stopped by the East 51st Street firehouse to chat with the firefighters, sometimes twice a week. He talked with them about their jobs, their families, their hopes and dreams. And about the loss of their colleagues. They talked about war. Vonnegut, a prisoner of war during the bombing of Dresden in 1945, spoke with Captain Dudley about Dudley's father, who served in the same war. Firefighters remember that Vonnegut paid his last visit to the firehouse in late March 2007. Just a few weeks later, the noted author, supportive neighbor, and friend to so many in the Turtle Bay community, died at the age of 84.

"I have a great admiration for firemen," Vonnegut said shortly before his death. Recalling the night in early 2000 when firefighters helped him out of his burning house, he said, "I consider that a great honor."

The Willow Tree

In the late 1940s, many years before Vonnegut moved to the neighborhood, another Turtle Bay author, E. B. White, wrote *Here is New York*, an essay on the city he called "both changeless and changing." His prophetic prose, much quoted over the years, recalled the days when the Third Avenue El still rumbled along; when the United Nations—"City of Man," White called it—was only beginning its rise along Turtle Bay's riverfront; and when the city, now in a nuclear age, for the first time in its history was destructible. "A single flight of planes no bigger than a wedge of geese can quickly end this island fantasy. . ." he wrote. "The intimation of mortality is part of New York now."

Republished not long before September 2001, the 7,500-word *Here is New York* was read by multitudes of New Yorkers in the aftermath of the September 11 terrorist attacks. To many, White's insightful stroll through a New York of yesterday helped heal deep wounds and gave hope for the city and its people.

In closing his essay, White wrote:

> A block or two west of the new City of Man in Turtle Bay there is an old willow tree that presides over an interior garden. It is a battered tree, long suffering and much climbed, held together by strands of wire but beloved of those who know it. In a way it symbolizes the city: life under difficulties, growth against odds, sap-rise in the midst of concrete, and the steady reaching for the sun. Whenever I look at it nowadays, and feel the cold shadow of the planes, I think: "This must be saved, this particular thing, this very tree." If it were to go, all would go—this city, this mischievous and marvelous monument which not to look upon would be like death.[3]

REACHING FOR THE SUN

Well into the first decade of the 21st century, the aging willow tree—more battered still—lived on in its private garden setting in the midst of Turtle Bay. Its thick, gnarled trunk reflected the passage of years. Yet, with nourishment from the underground Turtle Creek and care from concerned residents who trim its wispy branches, the tree had adapted to life in the new millennium. So, too, had the surrounding neighborhood, as it faced a future of further transformation over the coming decades.

Luxury residential towers, while not new to Turtle Bay, were being built at an unprecedented pace. Along First and Second Avenues, prime locations, the few remaining low-rise structures were being demolished to make way for strikingly modern glass-wrapped apartments.

On the area's southern edge, the nine-acre site of the former Con Edison Waterside power plant was sold and its century-old buildings were razed, to be rezoned and converted to a complex of office and residential buildings. With ample public open space, a school, and retail outlets, the project has the potential to enhance Turtle Bay by replacing the former industrial blocks with a vibrant community.

The United Nations was beginning a massive project to renovate its aging 1950s headquarters complex, with completion expected by 2013. In the interim, much of the U.N. staff was to move to nearby rented offices, and the General Assembly and conference sessions to a large, two-story temporary structure being built on the U.N. Gardens.

Longer term, the need remained for additional permanent U.N. space, and the United Nations Development Corporation was looking at options, including building offices on the site of Robert Moses Playground, a patch of land eyed for U.N. facilities since the mid-1960s.

In tandem with development along Midtown's East River, many in the community saw an opportunity for a long-desired waterfront esplanade that would run from 38th Street to as far north as 63rd Street, a recreational amenity many believed could finally become reality in a neighborhood long lacking in parkland.

Preservation of the neighborhood's history and architectural character remained paramount to Turtle Bay, as residents sought to landmark culturally significant buildings and protect the community's tree-lined blocks of 19th-century brownstones and town houses for many generations to come.

One momentous project, first proposed in the 1920s, finally got under way in the spring of 2007 when ground was broken for the long-awaited Second Avenue subway. The first phase—from 96th to 63rd Street—was to be completed by 2013. Plans called for the new subway to eventually run from 125th Street to lower Manhattan, easing the overcrowded Lexington Avenue line and bringing subway service closer to the heart of Turtle Bay.

When Mayor Michael R. Bloomberg developed a long-range plan to guide New York City through the year 2030, he identified three broad challenges: the growing population, aging infrastructure, and a more unpredictable environment. The city will succeed in meeting these challenges, he said, only if all its citizens are directly involved in planning—as earlier generations did—for a better and more sustainable tomorrow.

More than 50 years after the Third Avenue El gave way to modern high-rise office towers and long since the United Nations first moved to the East River waterfront, the people of Turtle Bay could look back on decades of working together, preserving the best of their past while building for the future. Now, facing the greater challenges of a new century, they would continue to look ahead with, in White's words, a "steady reaching for the sun."

SOURCES

BOOKS

Barrett, Mary Ellin. *Irving Berlin: A Daughter's Memoir*. Simon & Schuster, 1994.

Bergreen, Laurence. *As Thousands Cheer: The Life of Irving Berlin*. Viking, 1990.

Delaney, Edmund T. *New York's Turtle Bay: Old and New*. Barre Publishers, 1965.

Detmold, Mabel. *The Brownstones of Turtle Bay Gardens*. East 49th Street Association, 1964.

Dolkart, Andrew S.; and Matthew A. Postal. *Guide to New York City Landmarks*. John Wiley & Sons, 2004.

Gordon, Ruth. *Myself Among Others*. Atheneum, 1971.

Gray, Christopher. *New York Streetscapes: Tales of Manhattan's Significant Buildings and Landmarks*. Harry N. Abrams, 2003.

Hawkins, Stuart. *New York, New York*. Wilfred Funk, Inc., 1957.

Hepburn, Katharine. *Me: Stories of My Life*. Random House, 1991.

Huxtable, Ada Louise. *Four Walking Tours of Modern Architecture in New York City*. Doubleday, 1961.

Jackson, Kenneth T. *The Encyclopedia of New York City*. Yale University Press, 1995.

Kanin, Garson. *Tracy and Hepburn; An Intimate Memoir*. Viking Press, 1971.

Lankevich, George J. *New York City: A Short History*. New York University Press, 2002.

Morella, Joe. *Paul and Joanne: A Biography of Paul Newman and Joanne Woodward*. Delacorte Press, 1988.

Moses, Robert. *Public Works: A Dangerous Trade*. McGraw Hill, 1970.

Pickrel, Debra. *A Day in Turtle Bay: 20 Sites to See.* Turtle Bay Association, 2005.

Stelter, Lawrence. *By the El: Third Avenue and its El at Mid-Century.* H&M Productions, 1995.

Stern, Robert A. M., et al. *New York 2000: Architecture and Urbanism between the Bicentennial and the Millennium.* The Monacelli Press, 2006.

——————. *New York 1960: Architecture and Urbanism between the Second World War and the Bicentennial.* The Monacelli Press, 1997.

Walker, Danton. *Guide to New York Nitelife.* Putnam, 1958.

White, E. B. *Here is New York.* Harper & Bros., 1949.

——————. *The Little Bookroom.* 1999.

——————. *Letters of E.B. White* (edited by Dorothy Lobrano Guth). Harper & Row, 1976.

White, Norval; and Elliot Willensky. *AIA Guide to New York City.* The MacMillan Company, 1967, 1968. Three Rivers Press, 2000.

Wolfe, Gerard R. *New York: A Guide to the Metropolis.* McGraw Hill, 1994.

WPA Federal Writers Project. *New York City Guide.* Random House, 1939.

PERIODICALS AND OTHER

The New York Times
New York *Daily News*
New York Herald Tribune
New York Observer
New York Post
Newsday
The Wall Street Journal
Architectural Digest, December 1980; May 1992
District Lines, Historic Districts Council, Winter 2002
Holiday Magazine, May 1955
Pan Am Clipper Newsletter, March 1977

Real Estate Record and Guide, January 14 and 21, 1893

The Daily Plant, City of New York Parks & Recreation Department, October 6, 1987

Turtle Bay Gazette and Newsletter, Turtle Bay Association

Document Services, City of New York Parks & Recreation Department

Landmarks Preservation Commission Designation Reports, Nos. 6 and 7, June 21, 1966

New York School of Interior Design News, 2006

Plan for Development, Fund for Area Planning and Development, April 1968

The UN Center: A Development Program for UN Related Activities, UNDC, November 1969

INTERVIEWS AND CONVERSATIONS

Research for *Manhattan's Turtle Bay* included interviews and conversations with the following: Lewis Baer, Ellen Blair, Bradford Billet, Bronson Binger, Detective Frank Bogucki, Toni Carlina, Rita Carpanini Thompson, Steve Corvi, Colleen Curtis, John Detmold, Captain William Dudley, Donald Elliott, Georges Faber, Jeffrey Feldman, Mari Fransson, Peter Gabelli, Katherine Grenier, Carol Greitzer, Dorothy Lobrano Guth, George Hambleton, Dennis Herman, Alex Herrera, Elinor Jay, Melvyn Kaufman, Simeon Klebaner, Brenda Levin, Archibald King, Marion King, Michael Lucas, Shirley MacLeod, Robert Moyer, Prue Bach Mortimer, Nancy Ost, Nancy Owens, Angela Paolini, Gary Papush, Irene Peveri, Buddy Radisch, Paul Selver, Lou Sepersky, Andrew Smith, Stephen Sondheim, Erik Stapper, Edmund "Ted" Stanley, Henry Stern, Vivian Van de Perre, Thomas Romich, George Vellonakis, Kurt Vonnegut, John Wallowitch, and countless other Turtle Bay residents.

In addition, conversations with the members of the Turtle Bay Association Board of Directors were invaluable: Jed Abrams, Ethel Bendove, Bunny Blei, Meryl Brodsky, Orin Buck, Barbara Connolly,

Sources

Bill Curtis, Denise Hamilton, Marie-Louise Handal, Olga Hoffmann, Bill Huxley, Francine and Richard Irwin, Millie Margiotta, Dolores Marsh, Patricia Q. McDougald, Michael Resnick, Carol Rinzler, Jeannie Sakol, Helen Shapiro, and Bruce Silberblatt.

PERMISSIONS